To My Daughter
ELLEN JEAN

TWENTIETH CENTURY INTERPRETATIONS
OF

THE RIME
of the
ANCIENT
MARINER

A Collection of Critical Essays

Edited by

JAMES D. BOULGER

Prentice-Hall, Inc.   *Englewood Cliffs, N. J.*

A SPECTRUM BOOK

Current printing (last number):
10 9 8 7 6 5 4 3 2 1

Prentice-Hall International, Inc. (*London*)

Contents

"The Rime of the Ancient Mariner"—
Introduction

by James D. Boulger

The outward life of Samuel Taylor Coleridge is easily presented, because his real life lies essentially in his mind and in his many and varied writings. The outward life was certainly not flamboyant, as in the case of Byron and Shelley, or of many of our modern writers; nor was it successful and satisfying in the worldly sense, as in the case of his friend Wordsworth and many of the eminent Victorians shortly to come. It was an outward life mainly of failure and humiliation. Born at Ottery St. Mary in Devonshire on October 21, 1772, the youngest son of a clergyman, Coleridge was sent up to London at age ten to Christ's Hospital, a scholarship school as we say today, and from there proceeded sizar to Jesus College, Cambridge in 1791. A distressing career followed, and an unsuccessful marriage in 1795 to Sara Fricker, sister of Edith Fricker who married his friend Robert Southey. A meeting with William Wordsworth in 1795 led to the happiest and most poetically productive years of his life, 1795–1802: the years of *Lyrical Ballads,* "The Ancient Mariner," "Kubla Khan," "Christabel," and much more. But by 1802 personal problems of many kinds led to the great "Dejection: An Ode," his swan song as a major poet. Thereafter, the breakup of his marriage, an unfortunate attachment to Sara Hutchinson, sister of Wordsworth's wife, ill health, and opium-taking led to a career of wandering, of living in others' houses, of embarrassment and ignominy.

Only a sampling of that wandering need be documented here. In 1804, after two desultory years in the Lake Country at Gretta Hall in Keswick, the marriage to Sara Fricker informally broken off, Coleridge left his wife and children in the care of the Southeys, who had moved in with them in that free and easy way that characterized the early comings and goings of Coleridge, Wordsworth, Southey, and their circle. An appointment at Malta promised a change of scene and perhaps a change of life. He returned to England in 1806, having also visited Sicily, Italy, Gibraltar, and other parts of the Mediterranean area. There are many interesting accounts in the Notebooks of this extended trip, but little of poetic merit survives these years. When he landed at Stangate Creek in Kent (August 17, 1806), he was a shattered man; the opium habit was more firmly in control than ever, and he could not face the thought of returning to his wife and family. The separation from Mrs. Coleridge was made formal, with the usual mixed arrangements for the children. From 1806 to 1816 was the nadir of Coleridge's life, a continual moving from the home of friend to friend in the country, or from hotel to hotel in London. Occasionally he was able to pull himself together, to give the Lectures on Shakespeare (1811–1812) in London, or to edit *The Friend* in the Lake District (1809). He became a difficult case for his friends, culminating in the famous break with Wordsworth in 1812. Wordsworth had spoken of Coleridge's general failure to an acquaintance, Basil Montagu, who later repeated the story to Coleridge. The exact words are a matter of dispute, since Wordsworth denied the story in the form that it came back to him. Whatever the exact words, he had hit the mark and Coleridge could forgive neither himself nor his friend for the tasteless expression of truth.

In 1816 a second lease on life was offered at Highgate, in the home and under the care of a physician, Dr. James Gilman. From there came an enormous outpouring of prose works of literary criticism, philosophy, politics, and religious thought until Coleridge's death in 1834. In the opinion of his contemporaries, he had never quite lived up to the high hopes held out for him in early youth. His own view of his life's work was more cheerful. And if we think of his life as essentially that of the mind, it is not difficult today to accept his judgment.

Coleridge's most brilliant poems were written between 1795 and 1802; of their reception and understanding by the general public, something will be said in considering the history of "The Ancient Mariner." As a literary critic (*Biographia Literaria,* 1817) and commentator on the life of the times (*The Friend,* 1809; *Church and State,* 1829) he achieved greater recognition and understanding in his lifetime than he did as transmitter of German philosophy to the English world (*Philosophical Lectures,* 1818) or as a religious philosopher and thinker (*Aids to Reflection,* 1825; *Confessions of an Enquiring Spirit,* 1828), areas in which his thinking was not readily understood, and even became the object of contemporary ridicule. Yet it is precisely in these latter areas, and in the poetry, that Coleridge speaks most readily and forcefully to us. His public purpose and stated aim in his last years was "to provide a safety lamp for religious inquirers," particularly for Christians worried about the problem of belief and faith. In itself this may not be a great recommendation to readers of today, smacking as it does of pastoral letters to a flock. But the doubts and questions Coleridge raised were not those of his own century; they were of ours. His contemporaries on the whole failed to understand his questions and were puzzled by his answers and formulations; today, though we may not be able to accept his formulations, wherever we question (in the novel, in philosophy, in aesthetic theory, in political theory), we find Coleridge has been there before us. It is his searching mind, his inquiring spirit that is an image of our own and may yet be several steps ahead.

This aspect of Coleridge is central to our understanding "The Ancient Mariner," an epic in miniature of his life's work. In its symbolic structure it contains the searchings, questions, and tentative solutions of many years of speculation. In the nineteenth century only the astute Sir Leslie Stephen noted this, when he said,

> The germ of all Coleridge's utterances may be found—by a little ingenuity—in the "Ancient Mariner." For what is the secret of the strange charm of that unique achievement? I do not speak of what may be called its purely literary merits. . . . I leave such points to critics of finer perception and a greater command of superlatives. But part, at least, of the secret is the case with which Coleridge moves in a world of which the machinery (as the old critics called it) is supplied by the mystic philosopher.[1]

In a sense modern criticism of the poem can be looked upon as a following through of Stephen's insight.

Before turning to some of that modern criticism, which began with the publication of Lowes' *The Road to Xanadu* in 1927, we ought to look briefly at the earlier history of the poem. If it was misunderstood and neglected in its symbolic and central meaning, this is by no means to say that it was neglected or unknown, like the major works of Blake, until our own century. Indeed a great deal of ballyhoo surrounds the origin, publication, and reception of the poem in the nineteenth century. This fact is due in no small way to the considerable abilities of Wordsworth and Coleridge as publicists of their own work, and to the fact that "The Ancient Mariner," composed in 1797–98, appeared first in the famous *Lyrical Ballads* of 1798 and 1800. In the *Biographia Literaria* of 1817 Coleridge discussed at length the circumstances surrounding the publication of *Lyrical Ballads* and the composition of "The Ancient Mariner," and he was not averse to referring to the poem in his *Table Talk* (published in 1835) and elsewhere. The *Lyrical Ballads* were to be a reaction to decayed neoclassical

[1] Leslie Stephen, *Hours in a Library* (London, 1892), III, 358.

norms of the 1790's, and, in Coleridge's portion, an attempt to put
the current rage for sensational Gothic and supernatural materials to
better use. In his own famous words:

> . . . it was agreed, that my endeavours should be directed to persons
> and characters supernatural, or at least romantic; yet so as to transfer
> from our inward nature a human interest and a semblance of truth
> sufficient to procure for these shadows of imagination that willing
> suspension of disbelief for the moment, which constitutes poetic faith.[2]

From the time of first publication of the poem in 1798, the central
problem has always involved how seriously and in what sense to take
the key passage, "persons and characters supernatural, or at least
romantic." Wordsworth criticized the poem on grounds of character
and probability, and disliked many of the Gothic elements. Some of
these were toned down or omitted in the 1800 and subsequent editions
of the *Lyrical Ballads,* and Coleridge was induced to add to the title,
"A Poet's Reverie." The 1817 version in *Sibylline Leaves,* in which
the Gloss appears for the first time, omitted several of the more glaring Gothic incidents. This has become our standard edition of the
poem. There is no doubt that Coleridge was defensive about the poem,
and disappointed that it was taken merely as a voguish gothic tale
after the manner of Bürger's *Lenore* and Scott's *The Wild Huntsman*
(to both of which it does owe surface debts of an obvious kind). But
his adding of the Gloss in 1817, and his persistence in referring to it
in his literary discussions and other prose also leave no doubt that he
came to see this poem as central to his life of the mind, if he did not
already do so at the time of composition. In an age of literalists and
simple moralists, however, he was content to give the kind of answer
to the question of its meaning that a person of Mrs. Barbauld's in-
telligence and viewpoint might understand:

> Mrs. Barbauld once told me that she admired the Ancient Mariner
> very much, but that there were two faults in it,—it was improbable, and
> had no moral. As for the probability, I owned that that might admit
> some question; but as to the want of a moral, I told her that in my
> own judgment the poem had too much; and that the only, or chief
> fault, if I might say so, was the obtrusion of the moral sentiment so
> openly on the reader as a principle or cause of action in a work of such
> pure imagination.[3]

This was the same Coleridge who expounded the inner meaning of
the poem to friends during a walking tour of Germany in 1798–99.[4]

[2] *Biographia Literaria,* ed. J. Shawcross (London, 1907), II, ch. xiv.
[3] *Table Talk* (1835). May 31, 1830.
[4] C. Carlyon, *Early Years and Late Reflections* (London, 1836, 1858), I, 138–39.

In short, the poem received an extraordinary amount of attention in the nineteenth century, and if it was not fully understood, or was badly interpreted, Coleridge had no reason to expect a better audience. It met the fate of all symbolist and idealist poetry in a rationalistic and scientific age.

As Foster Damon's *William Blake* (1924) began the modern study and understanding of that neglected symbolist and artistic genius, so we may say that John Livingstone Lowes' *The Road to Xanadu*[5] revived the serious study of Coleridge's major poetry. But there was a crucial difference. Damon was a serious reader of Blake's symbolic world, whereas Lowes was mainly interested in finding the literary sources of "The Ancient Mariner," "Kubla Khan," and the other poems. Lowes' definition of Imagination and his estimate of "The Ancient Mariner" meet no contradiction with the enforced subtitle in the 1800 edition of *Lyrical Ballads*, "A Poet's Reverie." Although it has been fashionable to underestimate Lowes' contribution to Coleridge criticism in recent years, we must admit that his work laid a foundation of interest in the poem, and provided the vast knowledge of the sources of the poem in Coleridge's omnivorous reading that has helped later readers to fathom the symbolic meaning more fully. It would not be possible to repeat Lowes' findings in this short introduction, except to say that his book firmly established the sources for the major images and scenes in the poem—the mariner, the albatross, the voyage, the water snakes, much of the supernatural machinery— in two kinds of popular eighteenth-century reading, travel books of exploration and discovery, and popular ballads of the day. Since the poem is in form an adaptation of the popular and literary ballad (Percy's *Reliques* were published in 1765, and German ballads were translated into English later in the century) this is as it should be. Even if we accept as a literary truism that a source is not a meaning, we can agree that Lowes' monumental work was the foundation, the beginning, of serious modern study of Coleridge's poetry.

In genre "The Ancient Mariner" must be called a ballad, although it is unique in ballad literature and shares more qualities with epic than with ballad tradition. There is abundant evidence in the Notebooks, Letters, and elsewhere[6] that Coleridge contemplated an epic in the late 1790's (as indeed he continued to do throughout his life), and, while there is no evidence that he considered "The Ancient Mariner" an epic in miniature at the time of original publication,

[5] J. L. Lowes, *The Road to Xanadu* (Boston, 1927).

[6] *The Notebooks of Samuel Taylor Coleridge*, ed. Kathleen Coburn (New York, 1957, 1961) ; *Collected Letters of Samuel Taylor Coleridge*, ed. E. L. Griggs (Oxford, 1956, 1959). Passages are too numerous to quote here in full.

there is much evidence that with hindsight he came to view the poem
as a short symbolist epic. This is an important point, for it allows us
to appreciate the complicated provenance and structure of the poem.
The debt to ballad tradition is plain in the meter, in the archaisms
of the first version which appeared in *Lyrical Ballads,* in the swift
pacing of events, and in some of the more glaring Gothic elements.
This passage, for instance, widely criticized by friends, was omitted
from the *Sibylline Leaves* text of 1817, and is therefore not today a
part of the general reader's experience of the poem:

> I turn'd my head in fear and dread,
>   And by the holy rood,
> The bodies had advanc'd, and now
>   Before the mast they stood.
>
> They lifted up their stiff right arms,
>   They held them strait and tight;
> And each right-arm burnt like a torch,
>   A torch that's borne upright.
> Their stony eye-balls glitter'd on
>   In the red and smoky light. (489–498)

Here is the charnel house atmosphere we associate with the Gothic
novels of the 1790's, with Walter Scott's *Ballads from the German,*
and with the more supernatural of the English and Scottish border
ballads, all of which gave delight to the popular mind of the time.
However, we have learned from Lowes, J. B. Beer, and others that the
most striking and enduring supernatural elements came not from
ballad sources, but rather from Coleridge's wide reading in travel
literature, in Neoplatonic and other occult traditions, and from certain philosophers, particularly Berkeley. For this reason the sense of
the poem as a ballad, though true in part, gives way to a greater sense
of the poem as a peculiar example of the epic tradition.

It would be presumptuous and vain in this introduction to retrace
Coleridge's wide reading, and the wide reading of the scholars who
have followed in his steps, tracking sources for the albatross, the
Mariner, and other striking images and pieces of supernatural machinery in the poem.[7] Two prominent examples must suffice, Lowes'
tracing of the albatross to Captain George Shelvocke's *Voyage round
the World by the way of the Great South Sea* (London, 1726) and
J. B. Beer's discovery of a strikingly close source for the Mariner, more
convincing than the general idea of the "Wandering Jew" put forth
by Lowes, in Richard Hole's *Remarks on the Arabian Nights' Enter-*

---

[7] *The Road to Xanadu, op. cit.* J. B. Beer, *Coleridge the Visionary* (London, 1959).

tainments (1797).[8] In these sources and many more the scholars have sensed Coleridge's search for original images and patterns as his own equivalent of the epic events and machinery of the past. We know that he was reading the *Aeneid* and *Paradise Lost* afresh in 1796 and 1797,[9] and echoes from Virgil's epic appear in the poem. More profound is the relationship between "The Ancient Mariner" and the *Odyssey,* a relationship not of surface effects and machinery but of the inner or "occult" meaning of the symbols. Thomas Taylor, whose translations of Plato and the Neoplatonists in the late eighteenth century gave impetus to the idealistic thinking of Blake as well as Coleridge, published in 1788 *Philosophical and Mathematical Commentaries of Proclus,* in which appeared a very full Neoplatonic allegory of the wanderings of Ulysses, of which a short example here must suffice:

> . . . Ulysses after a voluntary submission to his natal daemon, by indulging the irrational appetites and desires of his soul, flies from his base servitude; and adds irritations to his flight. He is, however, pursued by the anger of the marine and material daemons, and punished for his escape. For he who blinds the eye of sense, and extinguishes its light, after his will has profoundly assented to its use, must expect punishment for the attempt; as necessary to his own private good, and the general order of the universe. Indeed, troubles and misfortunes resulting from such undertakings, not only contribute to appease the anger of their malevolent authors, but likewise purify and benefit the subjects of their revenge.[10]

The closeness of this interpretation to the Gloss added by Coleridge in the *Sibylline Leaves* edition of 1817, and to the theme of wandering, punishment, and salvation agreed upon by all major commentators on the poem will be obvious. In short, "The Ancient Mariner" is Coleridge's "brief epic," whether originally planned that way or not. It is a ballad of strange and supernatural events on the surface, and has quite legitimately engaged many generations of readers on that level. In our century there has also been endless speculation and much debate as to the inner, or "occult" meaning of the poem in Neoplatonic terms, and the open question of how far Coleridge intended that meaning. To these matters we must now turn.

[8] J. B. Beer, *Coleridge the Visionary* (London: Chatto & Windus, 1959), p. 146. The entire chapter on "The Ancient Mariner" in this book ("The Glorious Sun," Chap. V, 133–74) is excellent and is not reprinted in this volume for reasons of space.

[9] *Notebooks,* I, *op. cit.,* entry nos. 174, 311, and notes to these numbers.

[10] T. Taylor, *Philosophical and Mathematical Commentaries of Proclus,* 1788, II, 295n.

The major essays in this volume have been selected to discuss precise questions of theme and structure in "The Ancient Mariner." All the important matters—the primary theme of guilt, punishment, and redemption; the secondary theme of Imagination and the artist's vision; structural questions regarding the journey, the characters, supernatural machinery, "occult" symbolism, and the "moral" ending, to name the most striking—are considered in detail by Warren, House, Whalley, and Buchan, significant commentators on the poem. The moot questions, and disagreements thereon, will become obvious to the reader as he moves through the essays. For this reason what follows here as introduction to the poem's meaning is not intended as another specialist reading, or an attempt to adjudicate among the readings, but rather as a general frame of reference for readers of the poem and the essays, since a good consensus does exist as to the major themes and most important structural questions in the poem.

The two major themes in the poem might be called the creation of a sacramental universe by means of creative imagination and the operation within that universe of the religious pattern of Fall and Redemption. Thus the two most interesting ideas in the poem are the nature of the Will and the nature of Imagination. But there is much more, and there are many interrelationships among the major themes. Since Lowes at least, critics have noticed the dreamlike quality of much of the poem—it is an element of structure related to the epic journey pattern of *The Odyssey, The Aeneid,* and *Paradise Lost*; as an element of theme it is important in the dramatization of primary imagination in the poem. The epic quest pattern of the Mariner's search has interesting parallels in Homer, Virgil, and Milton, many of which illuminate the religious character of the Mariner's quest.[11] In the matter of pure structure, the albatross, water snakes, and Polar Spirit are obviously symbolic figures; so also are the sun, the moon, and stars in many appearances linked variously with the Fall-Redemption theme or with the aesthetic and philosophical cluster of terms which add meaning to the poem—Primary imagination, Secondary imagination, fancy, Reason, understanding. From the mingling of themes at the end of the poem, another theme, the creative artist and his place in the actual world, emerges as perhaps the most fascinating to the modern reader. Other possible themes are more tentative, "allegorical" if you will, and their place in the poem has been hotly disputed. The Mariner may be a Necessitarian or a secularized Calvinist, or he may be a Christian sceptic, illustrating the difficult

[11] James D. Boulger, "Christian Skepticism in 'The Rime of the Ancient Mariner,' " in *From Sensibility to Romanticism* (New York, 1965), pp. 439–52.

problem of knowing in parable form. A tantalizing view of the structure occurs in J. B. Beer's *Coleridge the Visionary*;[12] if one grants Coleridge's Neoplatonic and occult speculations and erudition, an occult meaning may be given to symbols such as the albatross and the water snakes going far beyond the level of Coleridge's usual rational discourse in *Biographia Literaria* and *Aids to Reflection* on religious and aesthetic subjects. Such meaning would derive from Proclus, Plotinus, and Egyptian mythological lore. The more speculative readings may appeal to some readers more than to others. What is clear is that the status of such readings in no way impairs the general parables of guilt-redemption and imagination-speculation central to the structure and meaning of the poem.

Let us see how these general thematic materials work together in a brief analysis of the structure of the poem. We may not assume that the cluster of moon symbols consistently represents the workings of imagination, or the sun symbols the discursive reason (Coleridge's prose understanding) and a form of alienation, but only that Imagination and understanding are present in the poem in various ways. The epistemology of the act of cognition in the poem is quite different from our everyday mode of perceiving the world, and from our usual way of reading poems. Coleridge's conception of the Imagination as a participation in the great I Am (and of the understanding used alone as the faculty which partakes of death) is to be taken quite seriously as the shaping force of the poem. Our nearest contemporary prose analogue is the philosophical system of symbolic form developed by Ernst Cassirer,[13] which holds that philosophy can only describe phenomena and must give up the attempt to understand causality or things. Neither this system, however, nor Coleridge's own descriptions of primary imagination in early nineteenth-century philosophical terms can be our primary guide. It is better to notice how things work out in the poem itself. For instance, understanding and syllogistic logic will be inferior categories to the higher level of imaginative perception in the action of the poem, without either being explained fully. The sailors use syllogistic logic and cause and effect in the ordinary way to calculate the morality of shooting the albatross, and of course the calculations fail, because the poem deals with effects whose causes are spiritual but unknown.

Ordinary reason and our dualistic world of sense perception are inoperative in the main body of the poem, after the beginning of the main narrative. Intuition and a sense of the world as continuum and

[12] *Coleridge the Visionary, op. cit.*, pp. 133–74.
[13] Ernst Cassirer, *The Philosophy of Symbolic Forms*, 3 vols. (New Haven, 1953).

flux replace these usual perspectives and modes of thought (in which we distinguish ourselves from the object perceived, and perceive each object as a separate entity). This change begins with the lines,

> The ship was cheered, the harbour cleared
> Merrily did we drop . . .

But we should not, and really cannot in the unfolding of the poem, "plug in" categories of Coleridge's philosophical prose to define the atmosphere and logic of the poem. To know that "intuition" in the poem corresponds to the mystical "eye of reason" of Coleridge's prose does not lessen in any way the great imaginative mysteries of the poem or even the minor matters of "machinery." We can detect a hierarchy of categories (Imagination, fancy, Reason, understanding, etc., known from the prose) but have no easy way to explain how they work to give the poem its startling originality of atmosphere and events. On the other hand we must bring our sense of common logic to the central sections of the poem, even though it is of little aid in understanding these sections. For if we question the events and the imagery in this ordinary way, the poem will break up in inconsistencies. Yet we cannot leave our desire for logic and consistency completely behind as we read the poem. The poem, an act and illustration of creative imagination, evokes our own powers of "primary imagination," in Coleridge's terms. In Lowes' terms, which are more available than Coleridge's to most readers, our memories of dreams, states in which the senses and the conscious space-time restrictions inculcated by the reasoning process weaken, allowing the preconscious state of pure imagination latent in our minds to reassert itself, are the sounder guide to the prerational sense of the world of "The Rime of the Ancient Mariner." If this is the case, the tension between imagination and reason in the events and symbols of the poem has a counterpart in the mind of the reader.

The main body of the poem, then, despite some residue of logic and sense realism of our ordinary kind, is a world of "pure imagination" and will have the logic of a Dream, in so far as we can understand such logic. It is of help to know Coleridge's terms, which are used and explained in many of the essays within, but one can proceed more faithfully to the poem without exact abstract definition. In fact, exact philosophical definition has led to extreme views, since too exact definition distorts rather than explains the poem. The poem does not present an irrational world, as one school has it, nor a complete sacramental vision which implies a rational orderly way of looking at reality from a clear Christian perspective, as conservative critics unfamiliar with romantic vision have stated. Such readings tend to fulfill the definitions used by their authors, not the spirit of the poem. Archetypal patterns, brought to the poem in the study of Maud Bodkin,[14] fail also to explain anything beyond their own logic and inner consistency. The concept of Dream, however, not with specific archetypal content, but as defined by Lowes as the form, logic, movement, and shaping spirit of the poem, is useful as the best analogue to the imaginative process of the poem itself. In a way the reader plays the part of the wedding guest, is drawn into the central section of the poem unwillingly, and resists to some extent the unfolding of the poem with his understanding. When he begins to accept the point that understanding is not enough, that he must use his imagination to understand the poem, he begins to share in the central parable of the poem, which is of epistemological and religious import.

Let us set aside for the moment the nature of this religious and epistemological dimension of the poem, and turn to some examples of the tension between imaginative process and worldly logic in the central section, as illustration of what has been said thus far. The most obvious example, the confused moral reasoning of the sailors when faced by the unknown spiritual forces, was mentioned earlier. At the very beginning of the poem the difference between the outside logical world and the inner imaginative world is brought out sharply in the conflict between the actual order of the land world and the imaginative dreamlike world of the voyage and the sea. The wedding, its festivities, and the anxiety of the Wedding Guest all fall within the ordinary world of sense and logic. The Wedding Guest is a reasonable man, so he thinks; he wants reasons for things, but the Mariner has none to give. He also wants to participate in a function of the actual order, while the Mariner has only his dream to offer, "There was a ship." The arbitrary *givenness* of both the Mariner and his adventure has been noted by most commentators. For a short while the two worlds compete, with the orderly rational world of conventional bride and wedding gaiety gradually giving way to the phantom ship, its sudden voyage, and the living sun and moon. The Mariner's glittering eye, which might be called the eye of the higher reason which surpasses understanding, transforms the Guest until the noise and conviviality of the actual world with its logic and causality are replaced by the living world of primary imagination, by the silent white seas of the prerational pure imagination, in which the Mariner's voyage took place. The Wedding Guest is agonized—"I fear thee, Ancient Mariner"—as his world slips out from under him.

In the world of Imagination in which the voyage takes place four

[14] Maud Bodkin, *Archetypal Patterns in Poetry: Psychological Studies of Imagination* (Oxford, 1934).

aspects are noticeable, as evidence that the world of the poem is quite different from the land world—

1. the "Dream" quality of the voyage and all its events, with the participation of reality, living and nonliving in one organic whole, and the unending series of shifts between subjects and objects, sights and sounds, in the phenomena of the perceived world;
2. a special kind of logic, or "non-logic" if you will, in the main events and symbols of the poem;
3. a machinery of "spirits" of various orders not found in the ordinary world;
4. a special definition of appearance and reality, substance and surface, developed in the descriptions of objects, especially the sea, during the voyage.

Taken together, this special world contributes to define the nature of the major parable (Fall, redemption, scepticism, spiritual will, and Faith) not by mere fiat and statement, but as the total poetic logic of the poem.

The world of primary Imagination is conveyed in immediate and existential ways, not in abstract definition of terms. The notable means are appeals to the state of dreams, which we all recognize as different from the ordinary waking world, and appeals to unusual combinations of sounds and sights acceptable in the world of the poem but certainly "confusing" if considered under normal circumstances. As the voyage begins, the Sun and Storm-Blast are both personified as HE, typical of the dream-state that animates all things, living and nonliving, good and malevolent. The strange noises of the ice, "It cracked and growled, and roared and howled" (61) are compared directly to the dream-state of sensation, "Like noises in a swound!" (62) The dream-state is appealed to directly many times to explain the mysterious actions of the poem:

> And some in dreams assurèd were
> Of the Spirit that plagued us so—   (131–132)

Later, as the Albatross falls off and the rain begins, the Mariner exclaims,

> Sure I had drunken in my dreams
> And still my body drank. (303–304)

Toward the end of the voyage, when the painful and almost impossible return to land is enacted, the dream-state is once more evoked, not as explanation, but as a way of reminding himself and the reader of the abnormal situation:

> But swift as dreams, myself I found
> Within the Pilot's boat. (554–555)

In this connection there is a passage in which strange and curious sounds reach the Mariner's ear, again after he has compared his state (Part V, line 303 quoted above) to a waking dream. The mixed and confused quality of the sounds deliberately calls up for the reader as well as the Mariner a state other than ordinary waking consciousness:

> Around, around, flew each sweet sound,
> Then darted to the Sun;
> Slowly the sounds came back again,
> Now mixed, now one by one.
>
> Sometimes a-dropping from the sky
> I heard the sky-lark sing;
> Sometimes all little birds that are,
> How they seemed to fill the sea and air
> With their sweet jargoning!
>
> And now 'twas like all instruments,
> Now like a lonely flute;
> And now it is an angel's song,
> That makes the heavens be mute.

All this is texture and atmosphere, of course, in our usual poetic terms. In terms of the poem, and Coleridge's intention, it is an evocation of primary Imagination (the living Power and prime Agent of all human Perception) preparing us to accept the central religious parable in the poem.

The fact that ordinary Logic (cause and effect sequence) does not operate during the voyage has been noted by all serious readers and critics. Otherwise the poem must be set down as merely ridiculous. In "real life" we expect a proportion between a cause and an effect— *i.e.*, if I work hard, then I should succeed; if I press the accelerator, the car will move faster; if I do serious wrong, I will be punished by society. These are comfortable connections, whether good or bad as sequences for the individual, because they give the expectancy by which we live. But this is not the way events work out in the poem. For instance, here is a "logical" sequence to consider: If I feed an Albatross, an ice-floe will break up; if I kill an Albatross, a ship will be stranded by malignant forces and two hundred men will be doomed to die; if, under chance appearance of the moon, I bless water snakes, I will be forgiven the "crime," and after many supernatural events, be returned to shore under sentence of everlasting penance. In this same context the sailors' ordinary logic in considering the killing of the bird was previously mentioned as very important, for their miscalculations are an obvious clue to the fact that ordinary logic does not operate, and is not supposed to operate, in the world of the poem.

Many explanations have been given for this strange state of affairs, some of the best in the essays within. Much that can be accepted will not need repeating here, particularly Warren's theory that gratuitous fall and redemption, fabled in the killing and the blessing, are the best parable of original sin that we have. However, if we are aware that Coleridge was an erudite and serious man, not a fool writing a pot-boiler for an audience of "Gothic" sensibility, one further point can be made concerning the function of Logic and cause-effect sequences in the events of the voyage.

Coleridge had read David Hume's *A Treatise of Human Nature* (1739) with great care, and was especially interested in Hume's theory of Causation. Hume refused to accept any inner necessity between a cause and an effect, or any divine or spiritual power in the universe giving inner logic to phenomenal sequences. For Hume, things happen in this or that way, and men call "cause-effect" that which habitually happens in the same way. Thus cause-effect and if-then sequences are habits, and Logic a statement of known custom or convention in the world. Coleridge, always looking for inner and spiritual causes for events and phenomena, could not accept Hume's argument, but he appreciated its devastating effect upon the philosophy of common sense, the logic of ordinary reality, and the onrushing "scientific method" of the eighteenth century:

> Mr. Hume—no one will suspect me of being an advocate of Mr. Hume's opinions, but I most assuredly do think that he was attacked in a very illogical not to say unhandsome manner both by Priestley and Oswald, and . . . by Beattie. . . . Mr. Hume had some right to say it was a great big lie in octavo as far as it referred to him; for it went on the ground that Hume did not believe there was any connection of cause and effect that man could act by, whereas it was a proud challenge to your proud dogmatists *who conceived all things to be the influence of their reason,* and particularly those . . . complete Lockeans who held that all knowledge was derived from the senses and that there was no reality in the senses, and he cut the matter short by calling on them to prove that the ideas of cause and effect have any reality at all.[15]

In the events of the voyage in "The Ancient Mariner" Coleridge constructs a series of cause-effect, if-then situations which mock the logic of common sense and custom. His purpose was not of course to illustrate Hume with test cases defying custom and common sense, but to point to the inner and spiritual condition of man's position in the Universe, a position and condition more true than that of rationalism,

[15] *Philosophical Lectures of S. T. Coleridge,* ed. Kathleen Coburn (London, 1949), pp. 202–3. My italics.

and more profound than Hume's scepticism of rationalism and orthodoxy.

In a general sense, the above also explains the appearance and use
of the celebrated "machinery" in the poem. The Storm-Blast, the
Polar Spirit, Nightmare Life-in-Death, and the "troop of spirits blest"
all defy the common sense view of "things," and also the more scientific, abstract, and rational view of things developed by Hume, or by
Locke and Priestley, other high priests of the eighteenth-century scientific mentality. These Spirits are not of the essence of the spiritual
order developed in the major parable of the poem, but rather are
leftovers of the primitive poetic imagination, mythopoeic and Neo-
platonist in origin. Yet their presence is useful in flaunting the "order"
of common sense rationalism *and* the naturalistic scepticism of Hume
and the scientists. If we may say that the if-then of science and common sense is surface causality in the poem, then the chain of Spirits
from the earlier Neoplatonic world might be called "middle" causes.
Interesting and exciting as poetic machinery, they mock surface causality by explaining no more or less than surface causality explains,
that is, nothing, yet they too lead to the parable of inner and spiritual
causes and essences which the poem is really about. The poet plays
sceptic to relieve us of scepticism and of banal acceptance of our
world. The Mariner and the readers will not be allowed affirmation
and a glimpse of truth until both have taken an honest voyage into
the unknown, accepted what is unknowable as such, and returned to
affirm the spiritual will. Scepticism of causality plays its part in af-
firming the force of the Mariner's insight:

> O Wedding-Guest! this soul hath been
> Alone on a wide wide sea:
> So lonely 'twas, that God himself
> Scarce seemed there to be.

Most subtle in the attack on rationalism and common sense during
the voyage is the way in which objects appear to the primary percipient, the Mariner. Here another attitude or human dogma, comfortable for ordinary life, is at stake, namely, that any *thing* is composed
of primary qualities, such as extension, weight, texture, etc. which
are its "substance," and of secondary qualities, such as shape, color,
etc. which are "accidents." Locke and Hume had attacked this traditional idea, while Berkeley in his *Principles of Human Knowledge*
(1710) tried to show that both primary and secondary qualities of
things exist in the mind of the percipient as phenomena, and while
there may be things or objects as such, such objects have no "substance" knowable to us. Thus for Berkeley the acceptance of the ap-

pearances of the visible world is an act of Faith, and only God is the supreme and unknowable Cause of the "sense manifold" that we see and live in. This viewpoint, sceptical, religious, and intellectual at once, was more congenial to Coleridge's mind than any other presented in the poem—common sense, scientific rationalism, crude mythopoeia, or simple orthodoxy—the alternatives represented by the wedding guest, the sailors, the Spirits and the Hermit respectively.

This idea that phenomena, not things or substances, are what we know and deal with is worked into the voyage by emphasis upon what Berkeley called the *secondary* qualities (light, sound, color) over the primary qualities (extension, weight, texture) in the description of objects on the voyage. This point cannot be shown and proved by any one instance, since the effect is cumulative—on the Mariner and on the reader. Before the Mariner can accept faith, repentance, and a true sense of the spiritual order behind phenomena or objects, he must be frightened out of the easy, vulgar, and commonplace assurance of the "reality" of things. *L'homme moyen sensuel* is comfortable in the world of things; the man of spiritual insight cannot be—he must accept things as *givens,* not as ultimates, in a spiritual order. In terms of poetic structure, this new perception is brought about by affixing color, light, or sound imagery to objects with little or no emphasis on texture, weight, and extension. As a "device" of poetry it can be called a trick, but in this context it serves a deadly serious purpose. The ice "came floating by/As green as emerald" (53–54), the ship is "As idle as a painted ship/Upon a painted ocean (117–118), the water snakes

> . . . moved in tracks of shining white
> And when they reared, the elfish light
> Fell off in hoary flakes.
>
> *   *   *
>
> Blue, glossy green, and velvet black
> They coiled and swam; and every track
> Was a flash of golden fire.   (274–281)

Near the very end, before the approach to land begins, there is this description of the bay in light and color:

> And the bay was white with silent light,
> Till rising from the same,
> Full many shapes, that shadows were,
> In crimson colours came.   (280–284)

In this visual strategy the appearances of the sea are most central and important during the voyage. It is seldom described as having depth,

and never wetness or coldness, all "primary" qualities related to substance. Almost always it appears in imagery of light or color:

> The water, like a witch's oils,
> Burnt green, and blue, and white. (129–130)

> The charméd water burnt alway
> A still and awful red. (270–271)

Even towards the end of Part VI, as the spell is breaking, this imagery
continues, "once more/I viewed the ocean green" (442–443). The
purpose of all this is clearly revealed in what the Mariner says shortly
after,

> O let me be awake, my God!
> Or let me sleep alway. (470–471)

He has learned something of the spectral nature of ordinary reality,
and the fact that visual phenomena hide, not reveal "substance." One
must give up all fetishes of the common sense, and of the scientific and
mythopoeic worlds to make contact with spiritual reality. It is a price
few are willing to pay. The most dramatic and grisly instance of the
spectral world of things comes with the description of the phantom
ship, which is an emblem of a universe spectral, unknowable, yet
immensely dangerous to complacent man:

> When that strange shape drove suddenly
> Betwixt us and the Sun.
>
> *   *   *
>
> And straight the Sun was flecked with bars,
> (Heaven's Mother send us grace!)
> As if through a dungeon-grate he peered
> With broad and burning face. (175–180)

This is the image of Satan laughing and cajoling the Mariner to ultimate scepticism and despair; it is the dark night, after custom has
been found wanting, and the ultimate test of the spiritual Will that
the Mariner survives by an act of faith alone, the blessing of the water
snakes. The later German phrase, *Blick ins Chaos,* is a fair description
of the state towards which this strategy draws the Mariner and the
reader. But the Mariner, as we know, survives, later to say, despite
the experience of scepticism and despair:

> O sweeter than the marriage-feast
> 'Tis sweeter far to me,
> To walk together to the kirk
> With a goodly company!

To walk together to the kirk
And all together pray. . . . (601–606)

Before his return to land, the Mariner has become a man of religious insight and spirituality. After the imaginative act of blessing
the water snakes, he no longer asks the wrong logical questions or
looks for the wrong things, but rather acts out his assigned role. It
does not matter on the return voyage whether the Polar Spirit or
the wind moved the ship, or whether the sun-moon patterns recur
with systematic consistency. In retrospect his narration becomes a
vast dream-parable, a voyage into the unknown, "We were the first
that ever burst/Into that silent sea" (105–106). The Mariner's transgression, by a gratuitous act of his Will, of the unity of the cosmos
is a necessary failing common to us all, which, as Warren's essay holds,
is why he can speak to us. The poet, however, speaks also of a world
we can envision (and he as poet can create) but not return to or live
in. The poetic world of ice and Albatross cannot be entirely con-
formable to rationalistic analysis *a posteriori,* and the poet has made
this a major point of the voyage. On the other hand, the analogy to
our dream-state, where the primary imagination is again partially in
control of our minds, is an entrance to the world of the sudden, unmotivated succession of images which appears in the action of the
voyage of the poem. The dream-state acts as an existential parable for
the proposition that our "real" world is appearance, and the world of
imagination and process a spiritual reality. Let us turn now to the
remarkable ending of the poem, the ending of Part VI and Part VII,
where the return to the land world is brought about.

This return to harbor and to land at the end is perhaps the most
shocking and difficult part to accept, because it is a return to the
ordinary world of sense realism and conventional order, and requires
an adjustment of Imagination to Reason again, the reverse of the one
required as we moved into the world of the poem. Yet Coleridge
manages to bring it off successfully. It is no surprise that the ship, the
bodies, and all the spirits disappear on the approach of the normal
order again. The Mariner's desire for ordinary Christian absolution
can be understood as a reassertion of the laws of logical thinking and
causality in his mind. His redemption *has* taken place in the world of
symbolic action, but does not have status on land. The basic problem
in this part of the poem is the possibility of successful confrontation
of the dream world with actuality. In a ghost story of the usual variety,
where things are not to be taken too seriously, such as Burns' "Tam
O'Shanter," one object is usually brought back to the ordinary world
as a sign of "proof" that the spirit-world existed. In this poem it is

the Mariner himself who is the living proof of a more serious and deeper moral order than ours, and this fact is disturbing to the normal rationalistic sensibility, which would rather cling to its own limited sense of order and convention. The ending is supposed to leave the author, reader, and Wedding Guest believing that the Mariner's voyage was a real one into the seas of the Imagination and that his haunting vision and intuitive knowledge are more valid and powerful than our everyday world. Because the world of vision does not adjust to the world of sense and understanding, either overwhelming it or frightening it away, this element of the poem has been difficult for some readers to accept. Life of the imagination extracts its toll, not only upon the Mariner and Wedding Guest, but upon the reader who learns that his own life, even in its most convivial and substantial forms, is a kind of alienation from deepest reality, and that the rational order of cause-effect and substance is merely a humanistic dream in an ocean of the unknown forces and causes that Berkeley, Coleridge, and the Neoplatonists had come to intuit. The Mariner's revelations, taken seriously, are a poison cup from which one never fully recovers again into normal perception. He assaults the sensibilities of the outside world, while at the same time suffering the penance of being forced again to live in the death-in-life world of the understanding and sense realism. He is a parable of the creative poet, of course, working in the modern rationalistic world, but he is not *maudit*, rather a necessarily suffering being, unless one is willing to grant that all creativity is an aberration.

Coleridge as poet was one of the first, with Blake, to envision this world of interrelated effects and of moral action unsupported by causes or a clear Divine cosmology. Like Blake, he did not like what he saw, but unlike him, he did not regard it as liberating the Imagination for a new humanism. The structure of "The Ancient Mariner" might be looked upon as that of classical epic, with a transformed epic framework and machinery of its own, but without the author's voice and authority to make the unknown and terrible orderly and rational. Coleridge plunges himself, his Mariner, and his readers into a seemingly arbitrary world of effects without logical causes, and of accidents (appearances) without substances, presented dramatically as Storms, hidden malignancy, human evils; yet finally he manages to suggest some a-rational, incredibly deep faith in the nature of things, analogous to that of the stumbling yet pious Aeneas. Later in life Coleridge was to find another analogy to this condition in the post-Kantian phase of Christian philosophy and theology. Deprived by Kant's *Critique of the Pure Reason* of "arguments from design," divine analogies and correspondences between the visible and invisible worlds—in short, of medieval and Renaissance rational arguments for religious belief—Christian philosophy and theology since Coleridge, Schleiermacher, and Kant have been less dogmatic and more a matter of Will and Faith.[16] A rational, pious will confronts a sceptical, unknowable universe, and thus, as in "The Ancient Mariner," there is an element of faith and an element of scepticism. Coleridge could never bring himself to publish his speculations on this subject, and, indeed, leaves the most daring of them in Greek or Latin.[17] Yet these speculations would provide a better gloss to the poem's meaning than the archly pious "moral ending" or the vague Gloss, which have misled commentators in various ways. Coleridge's excuse, also holding for Newton's speculations which remained and remain unpublished to this day, was that he was afraid of his own vision, or at least of a part of it. The world of "The Rime of the Ancient Mariner" is neither a clear presentation of a sacramental universe, nor a merely meaningless nightmare vision, but is rather an original parable in epic structure of the uneasy religious scepticism and faith that has been with us since Newton and Kant.

[16] For a full discussion of this, see James D. Boulger, *Coleridge as Religious Thinker* (Yale, 1961). The forthcoming *Collected Coleridge* (general editor, Kathleen Coburn) will have abundant primary evidence from Coleridge's hitherto unpublished prose writings of religious views and speculations.

[17] Marginalia to *Church of England Homilies*, 1815, in *Critical Annotations by S. T. Coleridge*, ed. William F. Taylor (Harrow, 1889). A striking example here, and numerous others in his marginal comments to the works of Jacob Boehme and eighteenth-century religious writers, could be cited.

PART ONE

Interpretations

A Poem of Pure Imagination:
An Experiment in Reading

by Robert Penn Warren

Part II

If *The Ancient Mariner* has a meaning, what is that meaning? . . .
In *The Ancient Mariner* I wish to distinguish two basic themes, both
of them very rich and provocative, and I shall, in the course of my
discussion, attempt to establish their interrelation.

One theme I shall call *primary,* the other secondary. I do not mean
to imply that one is more important than the other. But the one which
I shall call primary is more obviously presented to us, is, as it were, at
the threshold of the poem. The primary theme may be defined as the
issue of the fable (or of the situation or discourse if we are applying
this kind of analysis to a poem which does not present a fable). The
primary theme does not necessarily receive a full statement. In fact, in
The Ancient Mariner it receives only a kind of coy and dramatically
naïve understatement which serves merely as a clue—"He prayeth
best, etc." But the theme thus hinted at is the outcome of the fable
taken at its face value as a story of crime and punishment and reconciliation. I shall label the primary theme in this poem as the theme of
sacramental vision, or the theme of the "One Life." The operation of
this theme in the poem I shall presently explore.

As the primary theme may be taken as the issue of the fable, so the
secondary theme may be taken as concerned with the context of values
in which the fable is presented and which the fable may be found

From "The Rime of the Ancient Mariner, *A Poem of Pure Imagination: An Ex-
periment in Reading*" by *Robert Penn Warren. Condensed from* Selected Essays of
Robert Penn Warren (*New York: Random House, Inc.–Vintage Books, 1966*), *pp.
212, 213–14, 222–30, 231–50, 253–58, 262–63. Copyright* © *1946 by Robert Penn Warren. Abridged and reprinted by permission of the author and the publisher.*

ultimately to embody, just as more obviously it embodies the primary
theme. I shall label the secondary theme in this poem as the theme
of the imagination. After having explored the operation of the theme
of sacramental unity in the poem, I shall explore the operation of the
theme of the imagination, and shall then attempt to define the significance of their final symbolic fusion in the poem. . . .

Part III

. . . The fable, in broadest and simplest terms, is a story of crime
and punishment and repentance and reconciliation (I have refrained
from using the word *sin,* because one school of interpretation would
scarcely accept the full burden of the implications of the word). It is
an example, to adopt for the moment Maud Bodkin's term, without
necessarily adopting the full implications of her theory, of the archetypal story of Rebirth or the Night Journey. The Mariner shoots the
bird; suffers various pains, the greatest of which is loneliness and
spiritual anguish; upon recognizing the beauty of the foul sea snakes,
experiences a gush of love for them and is able to pray; is returned
miraculously to his home port, where he discovers the joy of human
communion in God, and utters the moral, "He prayeth best who
loveth best, etc." We arrive at the notion of a universal charity, which
even Babbitt admits to be "unexceptionable" in itself, the sense of the
"One Life" in which all creation participates and which Coleridge
perhaps derived from his Neoplatonic studies and which he had already celebrated, and was to celebrate, in other and more discursive
poems.

Such an account as the above, however, leaves certain questions un-
answered, and perhaps the best way to get at those questions is to consider the nature of the Mariner's transgression. Many critics, even
Lowes, for example, dismiss the matter with such words as *wanton,*
trivial, or *unthinking.* They are concerned with the act at the literal
level only. In substance, they ask: Did the Mariner as a man have a
good practical reason for killing the bird? This literal-mindedness
leads to the view that there is a monstrous and illogical discrepancy
between the crime and the punishment, a view shared by persons as
diverse in critical principles as Lowes with his aestheticism and Babbitt with his neo-humanistic moralism. But we have to ask ourselves
what is the symbolic reading of the act. In asking ourselves this
question, we have to remember that the symbol in Coleridge's view
is not arbitrary, but *must contain in itself, literally considered, the*
seeds of the logic of its extension—that is, it must participate in the

unity of which it is representative. And, more importantly in asking ourselves this question, we must be prepared to answer quite candidly to ourselves what our own experience of poetry, and life, tells us about the nature of symbolic import; and we must be prepared to abide the risks of the answer. It would be nicer, in fact, if we could forget Coleridge's own theory and stick simply to our own innocent experience. But that, at this date, is scarcely possible.

This question—what is the nature of the Mariner's act?—has received one answer in the theory advanced by Gingerich that the Mariner does not act but is constantly acted upon, that "he is pursued by a dark and sinister fate" after having done the deed "impulsively and wantonly" and presumably under necessity. For Gingerich's theory is that the poem is a reflection of the doctrine of necessity which much occupied Coleridge's speculations during the years immediately leading up to the composition of *The Ancient Mariner*: "I am a complete necessitarian, and I understand the subject almost as well as Hartley himself, but I go farther than Hartley, and believe the corporeality of *thought*, namely that it is motion." So the first problem we must consider is to what extent Coleridge was actually a necessitarian, at least in the poem.

It would seem that Gingerich has vastly oversimplified the whole matter, by choosing texts on one side of the question only, and sometimes by ignoring the context of a text chosen. He ignores, for example, the fact that even during the period when Coleridge professed devotion to Hartley he was under the powerful influence of his mystical studies (in Plato, Plotinus, Bruno, Boehme, etc.) and that looking back, in the *Biographia,* on his period of error he could say: "The writings of these mystics acted in no slight degree to prevent my mind from being imprisoned within the outline of any single dogmatic system. They contributed to keep alive the *heart* in the *head;* gave me an indistinct, yet stirring and working presentiment, that all the products of the mere *reflective* faculty partook of Death." And in the sentence quoted by Gingerich in which Coleridge proclaims himself a complete necessitarian, the context has been neglected: Coleridge proceeds to make a joke of the thrashing which "a certain automaton," Dr. Boyer, had visited upon one of his charges, a joke which indicates an awareness that the acceptance of the doctrine of necessity and materialism doesn't take the pain out of the offended buttocks. But to be more serious, it is possible to reach into another letter of the same general period, a letter to John Thelwall, in December, 1796, and find Coleridge saying flatly, "I am a Berkleyan." And this occurs in a long and passionate letter, really an essay, which is devoted to the attempt to convert Thelwall to Christianity; and in the course of the letter there is a fervid discussion of sin and repentance, concepts which Gingerich, extending certain texts from "Religious Musings" and other poems as a complete and tidy doctrine, denies to Coleridge. Gingerich even goes so far in his ardor to support his cause as to say that in "The Eolian Harp" (1795) Coleridge "conceives universal life as automatous," and proceeds to quote a few lines which in themselves might bear that interpretation. But he simply ignores the rest of the poem. The concluding stanza, which I shall present, follows immediately upon his chosen passage:

> But thy more serious eye a mild reproof
> Darts, O beloved Woman! nor such thoughts
> Dim and unhallowed dost thou not reject,
> And biddest me walk humbly with my God.
> Meek daughter in the family of Christ!
> Well hast thou said and holily disprais'd
> These shapings of the unregenerate mind;
> Bubbles that glitter as they rise and break
> On vain Philosophy's aye-bubbling spring.
> For never guiltless may I speak of him,
> The Incomprehensible! save when with awe
> I praise him, and with Faith that inly feels;
> Who with his saving mercies healèd me,
> A sinful and most miserable man,
> Wilder'd and dark, and gave me to possess
> Peace, and this Cot, and thee, heart-honour'd Maid!

Here the conclusion of the poem repudiates as "shapings of the unregenerate mind" the very statements by which Gingerich would argue for a relatively systematic necessitarianism. And we may note further in this passage that we find quite positively stated the idea of sin, a thing which, according to Gingerich, is not in the necessitarian system or in Coleridge's thought. But we can go to a direct, non-poetic statement in his letters, made just after the completion of *The Ancient Mariner*: ". . . I believe most steadfastly in original sin; that from our mother's wombs our understandings are darkened; and even where our understandings are in the light, that our organization is depraved and our volitions imperfect. . . ."

The point I wish to make is this: We cannot argue that Coleridge was a systematic necessitarian and that therefore the killing of the Albatross is merely the result of the necessary pattern of things and is not to be taken as sinful *per se* or in extension. The fact seems to be that Coleridge was early moving toward his later views, that he was not, as he says, committed to any dogmatic system, and that, as Shawcross points out, the poems themselves "are sufficient to show us that his professed adherence to the necessitarian doctrines of his day was by no means the genuine conviction of his whole being." As early as 1794, he was, we may add, thinking of the mind as an active thing, the "shaping mind"; and if, in one sense, we grant the power of mind we have broken the iron chain of necessity and the individual becomes a responsible agent and not the patient which Babbitt and Gingerich assume the Mariner to be. What A. E. Powell, in *The Romantic Theory of Poetry*, says of Wordsworth, that he lived his philosophy long before he phrased it, is equally true of Coleridge, and in addition to his living into a transcendental philosophy through the practice and love of poetry, he lived into the guilt of opium long before the Mariner shot the Albatross: he knew what guilt is, and if he longed for a view of the universe which would absolve him of responsibility and would comfort him with the thought of participation in the universal salvation promised by Hartley and Priestley, there was still the obdurate fact of his own experience.

We have in these years, it seems, a tortured churning around of the various interpretations of the fact, and the necessitarian philosophy is only one possble philosophy in suspension in that agitated brew. And we even have some evidence that in the period just before the composition of *The Ancient Mariner*—before he had struck upon that fable to embody his idea—the poet was meditating a long poem on the theme of the origin of evil. Early in 1797 Lamb wrote him: "I have a dim recollection that, when in town, you were talking of the Origin of Evil as a most prolific subject for a long poem." As a matter of fact, Coleridge never did "solve" his problem: he found peace simply by accepting the idea of Original Sin as a mystery.

In the *Table Talk* he says: "A Fall of some sort or other—the creation, as it were, of the non-absolute—is the fundamental postulate of the moral history of Man. Without this hypothesis, Man is unintelligible; with it every phenomenon is explicable. The mystery itself is too profound for human insight."

In his more elaborate and systematic treatment of the subject Coleridge adds another point which is of significance for the poem. Original Sin is not hereditary sin: it is original with the sinner and is of his will. There is no previous determination of the will, because the will exists outside the chain of cause and effect, which is of Nature and not of Spirit. And as for the time of this act of sin, he says that the "subject stands in no relation to time, can neither be in time nor out of time." The bolt whizzes from the crossbow and the bird falls and all comment that the Mariner has no proper dramatic motive or is the child of necessity or is innocent of everything except a little wantonness is completely irrelevant, for we are confronting the mystery of the corruption of the will, the mystery which is the beginning of the "moral history of Man."

The fact that the act is unmotivated in any practical sense, that it appears merely perverse, has offended literalists and Aristotelians alike, and, for that matter, Wordsworth, who held that the Mariner had no "character" (and we may elaborate by saying that having no character he could exhibit no motive) and did not act but was acted upon. The lack of motivation, the perversity, which flies in the face of the Aristotelian doctrine of *hamartia*, is exactly the significant thing about the Mariner's act. The act re-enacts the Fall, and the Fall has two qualities important here: it is a condition of will, as Coleridge says, "out of time," and it is the result of no single human motive.

One more comment, even though I have belabored this point. What is the nature of this sin, what is its content? Though the act which re-enacts the mystery of the Fall is appropriately without motive, the sin of the will must be the appropriate expression of the essence of the will. And we shall turn to a passage in *The Statesman's Manual*. Having just said that, in its "state of immanence or indwelling in reason and religion," the will appears indifferently as wisdom or love, Coleridge proceeds: "But in its utmost abstraction and consequent state of reprobation, the will becomes Satanic pride and rebellious self-idolatry in the relations of the spirit to itself, and remorseless despotism relatively to others . . . by the fearful resolve to find in itself alone the one absolute motive of action." Then he sketches the portrait of the will in abstraction, concluding with the observation that "these are the marks, that have characterized the masters of mischief, the liberticides, the mighty hunters of mankind, from Nimrod to Bonaparte."

We may observe a peculiar phrase, the "mighty hunters of mankind, from Nimrod to Bonaparte," and in this blending of the hunting of beasts and the hunting of man—for Nimrod was himself both the mighty hunter and the founder of the first military state—we have an identification that takes us straight to the crime of the Mariner. The Mariner did not kill a man but a bird, and the literal-minded readers have echoed Mrs. Barbauld and Leslie Stephen: what a lot of pother about a bird. But they forget that this bird is more than a bird. I do not intend, however, to rest my case on the phrase just quoted from *The Statesman's Manual*, for the phrase itself I take to be but an echo from the poem at the time when the author was revising and reliving his favorite poem. Let us go to the poem itself to learn the significance of the bird.

In the poem itself the same identification occurs: the hunting of the bird becomes the hunting of man. When the bird first appears,

> As if it had been a Christian soul,
> We hailed it in God's name.

It ate food "it ne'er had eat," and every day "came to the mariner's hollo," and then later perched on the mast or shroud for "vespers nine." It partakes of the human food and pleasure and devotions. To make matters more explicit, Coleridge adds in the Gloss the statement that the bird was received with "hospitality" and adds, after the crime, that the Mariner "inhospitably killeth the pious bird of good omen." The crime is, symbolically, a murder, and a particularly heinous murder, for it involves the violation of hospitality and of gratitude (*pious* equals *faithful* and the bird is "of good omen") and of sanctity (the religious connotations of pious, etc.). This factor of betrayal in the crime is re-emphasized in Part V when one of the Spirits says that the bird had "loved the man" who killed it.

But why did the poet not give us a literal murder in the first place? By way of answering this question, we must remember that the crime, to maintain its symbolic reference to the Fall, must be motiveless. But the motiveless murder of a man would truly raise the issue of probability. Furthermore, the literal shock of such an act, especially if perverse and unmotivated, would be so great that it would distract from the symbolic significance. The poet's problem, then, was to provide an act which, on one hand, would not accent the issue of probability or shockingly distract from the symbolic significance, but which, on the other hand, would be adequately criminal to justify the consequences. And the necessary criminality is established, we have seen, in two ways: (1) by making the gravity of the act depend on the state of the will which prompts it, and (2) by symbolically defining the bird as a "Christian soul," as "pious," etc.

There is, however, a third way in which the criminality is established. We can get at it by considering the observation that if a man had been killed, we could not have the "lesson of humanitarianism," which some critics have taken to be the point of the poem. But we must remember that the humanitarianism itself is a manifestation of a deeper concern, a sacramental conception of the universe, for the bird is hailed "in God's name," both literally and symbolically, and in the end we have, therefore, in the crime against Nature a crime against God. If a man had been killed, the secular nature of the crime—a crime then against man—would have overshadowed the ultimate religious significance involved. The idea of the crime against God rather than man is further emphasized by the fact that the cross is removed from the Mariner's neck to make place for the dead bird, and here we get a symbolic transference from Christ to the slain creature of God. And the death of the creature of God, like the death of the Son of God, will, in its own way, work for vision and salvation. . . .

To return to the problems raised by the poem: We have not yet done with the matter of crime and punishment. There is the question of the fellow mariners, who suffer death. Here we encounter not infrequently the objection that they do not merit their fate. The tragic *hamartia*, we are told, is not adequate. The Gloss, however, flatly defines the nature of the crime of the fellow mariners: they have made themselves "accomplices." But apparently the Gloss needs a gloss. The fellow mariners have, in a kind of structural counterpoint (and such a counterpoint is, as we shall see, a characteristic of the poem), duplicated the Mariner's own crime of pride, of "will in abstraction." That is, they make their desire the measure of the act: they first condemn the act, when they think the bird had brought the favorable breeze; then applaud the act when the fog clears and the breeze springs back up, now saying that the bird had brought the fog; then in the dead calm, again condemn the act. Their crime has another aspect: they have violated the sacramental conception of the universe, by making man's convenience the measure of an act, by isolating him from Nature and the "One Life." This point is picked up later in Part IV:

> The many men, so beautiful!
> And they all dead did lie:
> And a thousand thousand slimy things
> Lived on; and so did I.

The stanza is important for the reading of the poem. The usual statement for the poem is that the Mariner moves from love of the sea snakes to a love of men (and in the broad sense this is true), but here we see that long before he blesses the snakes he is aware, in his guilt, of the beauty of the dead men, and protests against the fact that the slimy things should live while the beautiful men lie dead. In other words, we have here, even in his remorse, a repetition of the original crime against the sacramental view of the universe: man is still set over, in pride, against Nature. The Gloss points to the important thing here: "He despiseth the creatures of the calm."

There is one other aspect of the guilt of the fellow mariners worthy of notice. They judge the moral content of an act by its consequence; in other words, they would make good disciples of Bishop Paley, who, according to Coleridge, in *Aids to Reflection,* was no moralist because he would judge the morality of an act by consequence and not "contemplate the same in its original spiritual source," the state of the will. The will of the fellow mariners is corrupt. And this re-emphasizes the fact that what is at stake throughout is not the objective magnitude of the act performed—the bird is, literally, a trivial creature—but the spirit in which the act is performed, the condition of the will.

So much for the crime of the Mariner and the crime of his fellows. And we know the sequel, the regeneration of the Mariner. In the end, he accepts the sacramental view of the universe, and his will is released from its state of "utmost abstraction" and gains the state of "immanence" in wisdom and love. We shall observe the stages whereby this process is consummated—this primary theme of the "One Life" is developed—as we investigate the secondary theme, the theme of the imagination.

Part IV

If in the poem one follows the obvious theme of the "One Life" as presented by the Mariner's crime, punishment, and reconciliation, one is struck by the fact that large areas of the poem seem to be irrelevant to this business: for instance, the special atmosphere of the poem, and certain images which, because of the insistence with which they are presented, seem to be endowed with a special import. Perhaps the best approach to the problem of the secondary theme is to consider the importance of light, or rather, of the different kinds of light.

There is a constant contrast between moonlight and sunlight, and the main events of the poem can be sorted out according to the kinds of light in which they occur. Coleridge underscores the importance of the distinction between the two kinds of light by introducing the poem by the motto from Burnet, added in the last revision of 1817 (in fact, the general significance of the motto has, so far as I know, never been explored). The motto ends: "But meanwhile we must earnestly seek after truth, maintaining measure, that we may distinguish things certain from those uncertain, day from night." The motto ends on the day-night contrast, and points to this contrast as a central fact of the poem. We may get some clue to the content of the distinction by remembering that in the poem the good events take place under the aegis of the moon, the bad events under that of the sun. This, it may be objected, reverses the order of Burnet, who obviously wishes to equate the "certain" or the good with day and the "uncertain" or bad with night. Coleridge's reversal is, I take it, quite deliberate—an ironical reversal which, in effect, says that the

rational and conventional view expressed by Burnet seeks truth by
the wrong light. In other words, Burnet becomes the spokesman of
what we shall presently find Coleridge calling the "mere reflective
faculty" which partakes of "Death."

Before we pursue this symbolism in the poem, let us look at moonlight in the larger context of Coleridge's work. Perhaps we shall find
that it is serving, not only in *The Ancient Mariner* but elsewhere,
the function defined by I. A. Richards: "When a writer has found a
theme or image which fixes a point of relative stability in the drift
of experience, it is not to be expected that he will avoid it. Such
themes are a means of orientation."

As for the moonlight, more than one critic has noted its pervasive
presence in Coleridge's work. Swinburne calls Coleridge's genius
"moonstruck." And even Irving Babbitt goes so far as to say: "A
special study might be made of the role of the moon in Chateaubriand
and Coleridge—even if one is not prepared like Carlyle to dismiss
Coleridge's philosophy as 'bottled moonshine.'" For the moon is
everywhere, from the "Sonnet to the Autumnal Moon" of 1788 on
through most of the poems, or many of them, trivial or great, sometimes with a specifically symbolic content, sometimes as the source of
a transfiguring light which bathes the scene of *Christabel* or *The
Ancient Mariner* or "The Wanderings of Cain" or "Dejection: An
Ode" or "The Nightingale" of 1798 or the deep romantic chasm of
"Kubla Khan," and always she is the "Mother of wildly-working
visions," as she is called in the sonnet mentioned, or the "Mother
of wildly-working dreams," as she is called in "Songs of the Pixies"
(1796). And in both the prose and verse, frequently when it is not
the moon in this role it is some cloudy luminescence, the "luminous
gloom of Plato," or "the slant beams of the sinking orb" of "This
Lime-Tree Bower," or the glitter of the sunlit sea seen through half-
closed eyelids in "The Eolian Harp."

We have, without question, a key image in Coleridge's moon, or
Coleridge's half-light, and Coleridge himself has given us, in sober
prose, a clue to its significance. Years later, looking back on the brief
period of creative joy and the communion of minds which marked
the years 1797 and 1798, he recalled the origin of the *Lyrical Ballads:*

> During the first year that Mr. Wordsworth and I were neighbours, our
> conversation turned frequently on the two cardinal points of poetry, the
> power of exciting the sympathy of the reader by a faithful adherence to
> the truth of nature, and the power of giving the interest of novelty by
> the modifying colours of the imagination. The sudden charm, which

accidents of light and shade, which moon-light or sun-set, diffused over
a known and familiar landscape, appeared to represent the practicability
of combining both. These are the poetry of nature.

Here the moonlight, or the dimming light of sunset, changes the
familiar world to make it poetry; the moonlight equates with the
"modifying colours of the imagination." To support this we have also
the account given by Wordsworth in the *Prelude* of the night walk
up Mount Snowden in the moonlight. . . . [63–86]

But to return to Coleridge's own testimony, not rarely we can find
the moon appearing in the prose. For instance, we may glance at this
passage in *Anima Poetae* on symbolism: "In looking at objects of
Nature while I am thinking, as at yonder moon dim-glimmering
through the dewy window pane, I seem rather to be seeking, as it
were *asking* for, a symbolic language for something within me that
always and forever exists, than observing any thing new." How easily
the moon, dim-glimmering, enters the conversation when his mind
turns to the imaginative relation of man and Nature.

Let us see how this symbol functions in the poem, in connection
with the theme of the imagination. We must remember, however,
that here by the imagination we mean the imagination in its value-
creating capacity, what Coleridge was later to call the secondary
imagination.

We shall not go far into the poem before we realize that the light
symbolism is not the only symbolism operating upon us. For instance,
we shall encounter winds and storms at various important moments.
Our problem, then, is not only to define particular symbolisms, but
to establish the relationships among them—to establish the general
import.

At the threshold of the poem, however, another consideration in-
trudes itself upon us. Certain images are first presented to us, and
sometimes may appear later, at what seems to be merely a natural
level. This question, then, will arise in the minds of certain readers:
How far are we to interpret, as we look back at the poem, such
apparently natural manifestations which at other times, at the great
key moments of the poem, are obviously freighted with significance?
In presenting the poem here I shall undertake the full rather than
the restricted interpretation. My reasoning is this: Once the import
of an image is established for our minds, that image cannot in its
workings upon us elsewhere in the poem be disencumbered, whether
or not we are consciously defining it. The criterion for such full
rather than restricted interpretation is consistency with the central

symbolic import and, in so far as it is possible to establish the fact, with the poet's basic views as drawn from external sources. We can derive no criterion from the poet's conscious intention *at any given moment in the poem,* and this question is, in this narrow sense, irrelevant. (In its broader sense, it will be discussed later in this essay.) In any case, though here I shall undertake a full interpretation, if a reader should wish to interpret the poem in a restricted sense, I would not feel that my basic thesis was impaired. There is always bound to be some margin for debate in such matters.

The problem of the fullness of interpretation presents itself to us at the very outset of the poem. The voyage begins merrily under the aegis of the sun. Is our sun here merely the natural sun, or is it also the symbolic sun? But the question is more acute a stanza or two on, when the storm strikes and drives the ship south, the behavior of the ship being described in the powerfully developed image of flight from a pursuing enemy. Is this a merely natural storm, or a symbolic one as well? Let us linger on this question.

Later in the poem we shall find wind and storm appearing as the symbol of vitality and creative force. A storm, we recall, strikes as a consequence of the Mariner's redemption and brings him the life-giving rain. Is the first storm, then, to be taken with the same force, even though it is presented here in the imagery of a terrible enemy? I do not find the import here inconsistent with that of the storm at the Mariner's redemption. The storm at the redemption, though a "good" storm, is also presented in imagery of terror and power. The ambivalence of the storm is an important feature which is extended and developed later in the poem. But for the present, merely glancing forward to that final interpretation of the wind and storm, we can say that the first storm is an "enemy" because to the man living in the world of comfortable familiarity, complacent in himself and under the aegis of the sun, the creative urge, the great vital upheaval, this "bottomwind," is inimical.

When the storm has driven the ship south, we reach the second stage of the Mariner's adventure, the land of ice. This land is both beautiful and terrible, as is proper for the spot where the acquaintance with the imagination is to be made. Like the storm which drives the ship south, it shakes man from his routine of life. Man finds the land uncomfortable; he loses his complacency when he confronts the loneliness:

> Nor shapes of men nor beasts we ken—
> The ice was all between.

But out of this awe-inspiring manifestation of Nature, which seems at first to be indifferent to man, comes the first response to man—the Albatross—to receive the glad "natural" recognition of the mariners.

I have already indicated how the bird-man fusion is set up, how the bird is hailed in God's name, etc., how, in other words, the theme of the "One Life" and the sacramental vision is presented. Now as a moment of great significance in the poem, I wish to indicate how the primary theme of the sacramental vision is for the first time assimilated to the secondary theme of the imagination. The Albatross, the sacramental bird, is also, as it were, a moon-bird. For here, with the bird, the moon first enters the poem, and the two are intimately associated:

> In mist or cloud, on mast or shroud,
> It perched for vespers nine;
> Whiles all the night, through fog-smoke white,
> Glimmered the white Moon-shine.

The sun is kept entirely out of the matter. The lighting is always indirect, for even in the day we have only "mist or cloud"—the luminous haze, the symbolic equivalent of moonlight. Not only is the moon associated with the bird, but the wind also. Upon the bird's advent a "good south wind sprung up behind." And so we have the creative wind, the friendly bird, the moonlight of imagination, all together in one symbolic cluster.

As soon as the cluster is established, the crime, with shocking suddenness, is announced. We have seen how the crime is to be read at the level of the primary theme. At the level of the secondary theme it is, of course, a crime against the imagination. Here, in the crime, the two themes are fused. (As a sidelight on this fact, we may recall that in "Dejection: An Ode," Coleridge gives us the same fusion of the moral and the aesthetic. In bewailing his own loss of creative power he hints, at the same time, at a moral taint. The "Pure of heart" do not lose the imaginative power, "this strong music in the soul.")

With the announcement of the crime, comes one of the most effective turns in the poem. As the Wedding Guest recoils from his glittering eye, the Mariner announces:

> . . . With my cross-bow
> I shot the Albatross.

And then the next line of the poem:

> The Sun now rose upon the right.

The crime, as it were, brings the sun. Ostensibly, the line simply describes a change in the ship's direction, but it suddenly, with dramatic violence, supplants moon with sun in association with the unexpected revelation of the crime, and with the fact indicates not only the change of the direction of the ship but the change of the direction of the Mariner's life. The same device is repeated with the second murder of the Albatross—the acceptance of the crime by the fellow mariners. They first condemn the Mariner for having killed the bird "that made the breeze to blow," but immediately upon the rising of the sun, they accept the crime:

> Nor dim nor red, like God's own head,
> The glorious Sun uprist:
> Then all averred, I had killed the bird
> That brought the fog and mist.

As has been pointed out earlier, the mariners act in the arrogance of their own convenience. So even their condemnation of the crime has been based on error: they have not understood the nature of the breeze they think the bird had brought. But here we must observe a peculiar and cunningly contrived circumstance: the mariners do not accept the crime until the sun rises, and rises gloriously "like God's own head." The sun is, symbolically speaking, the cause of their acceptance of the crime—they read God as justifying the act on the ground of practical consequence, just as, shall we say, Bishop Paley would have done. They justify the crime because the bird had, they say, brought the fog and mist. In other words, they repudiate the luminous haze, the other light, and consider it an evil, though we know that the fog and mist are associated with the moon in the wind-bird-moon cluster at the end of Part I.

At this point where the sun has been introduced into the poem, it is time to ask how we shall regard it. It is the light which shows the familiar as familiar, it is the light of practical convenience, it is the light in which pride preens itself, it is, to adopt Coleridge's later terminology, the light of the "understanding," it is the light of that "mere reflective faculty" that "partook of Death." And within a few lines, its acceptance by the mariners has taken them to the sea of death, wherein the sun itself, which had risen so promisingly and so gloriously like "God's own head," is suddenly the "bloody sun," the sun of death—as though we had implied here a fable of the Enlightenment and the Age of Reason, whose fair promises had wound up in the bloodbath of the end of the century.

In the poem, however, at this point where the agony begins, we find an instructive stanza:

And some in dreams assuréd were
Of the Spirit that plagued us so;
Nine fathom deep he had followed us
From the land of mist and snow.

This Polar Spirit, as the Gloss will call him later, is of the land of mist and snow, which we have found to be adjuncts of the wind-bird-moon cluster; hence he, too, belongs to the same group and partakes of its significance. Two facts stand out about the present "carrier" of the imagination: his presence is known by dreams and his errand is one of vengeance. The first fact tells us that the imagination, though denied or unrecognized, still operates with dire intimations at a level below the "understanding"; "understanding" cannot exorcise it and its subconscious work goes on. The second fact tells us that, if violated and despised, the faculty which should naturally be a blessing to man will in its perverted form exact a terrible vengeance.

The fellow mariners do not, of course, comprehend the nature of the Spirit whose presence has been revealed to them in dreams. They have learned, by this time, that a crime has been committed and that vengeance is imminent. But they do not know the nature of the crime or their own share in the guilt. So in their ignorance they hang the Albatross about the Mariner's neck. Thus the second major stage of the poem concludes.

Part III consists of two scenes, one of the sun, one of the moon, in even balance. The first is the appearance of the specter-bark, which is in close association with the sun. There is the elaborate description of the sun, but in addition there is the constant repetition of the word, five times within twelve lines:

1. Rested the broad bright Sun
2. Betwixt us and the Sun
3. And straight the Sun was flecked with bars
4. Are those *her* sails that glance in the Sun
5. Are those *her* ribs through which the Sun.

The whole passage, by means of the iteration, is devoted to the emotional equating of the sun and the death-bark.

Then the "Sun's rim dips," and we have the full and beautiful description of the rising of the "star-dogged Moon." But the moon does not bring relief; instead "At the rising of the Moon," as specified by the placement of the Gloss,

Fear at my heart, as at a cup,
My life-blood seemed to sip!

And immediately after, in the moonlight, the fellow mariners curse
the Mariner with a look, and, one after another, fall down dead.
The fact of these unhappy events under the aegis of the supposedly
beneficent moon raises a question: Does this violate the symbolism
of the moon? I do not feel that the poem is inconsistent here. First,
if we accept the interpretation that the Polar Spirit belongs to the
imagination cluster and yet exacts vengeance, then the fact that horror
comes in the moonlight here is simply an extension of the same
principle: violated and despised, the imagination yet persists and
exacts vengeance. Second, we find a substantial piece of evidence
supporting this view, in the parallel scene in Part VI, another scene
of the curse by the eye in moonlight:

> All fixed on me their stony eyes,
> That in the Moon did glitter.

But this parallelism gives us a repetition with a difference. This event
occurs after the Mariner has had his change of heart, and so now
when the curse by the eye is placed upon him in moonlight, it does
not avail; in moonlight now "this spell was snapt," and the creative
wind rose again to breathe on the Mariner. In other words, the
passage in Part VI interprets by contrast that in Part III. The moonlight, when the heart is unregenerate, shows horror; when the heart
has changed, it shows joy.

In Part IV the penance of loneliness and horror, both associated
with the crime against the imagination (loneliness by denial of the
imagination, horror by the perversion of it), is aggravated with the
despising of the creatures of the calm and with the curse in the eyes
of the dead. Then, suddenly, we have the second moonrise:

> The moving Moon went up the sky,
> And no where did abide:
> Softly she was going up,
> And a star or two beside—

The Gloss here tells us all we need to know, defining the Mariner's
relation to the Moon:

> In his loneliness and fixedness he yearneth towards the journeying
> Moon, and the stars that still sojourn, yet still move onward; and every
> where the blue sky belongs to them, and is their appointed rest, and
> their native country and their own natural homes, which they enter
> unannounced, as lords that are certainly expected and yet there is a
> silent joy at their arrival.

Life, order, universal communion and process, joy—all these things
from which the Mariner is alienated are involved here in the descrip-

tion of the moon and stars. And immediately the description of the water snakes picks up and extends the sense of the stars. The snakes become creatures of light to give us another symbolic cluster:

> They moved in tracks of shining white,
> And when they reared, the elfish light
> Fell off in hoary flakes.

For the Gloss says here: "By the light of the Moon he beholdeth God's creatures of the great calm." And in the light of the moon we have the stages of the redeeming process: first, the recognition of happiness and beauty; second, love; third, the blessing of the creatures; fourth, freedom from the spell. The sequence is important, and we shall return to it. In it the theme of the sacramental vision and the theme of imagination are fused.

Part V, in carrying forward the next period of development consequent upon the Mariner's restored imaginative view of the world, continues, in new combinations, the sun-moon contrast, but here we move toward it by the refreshing rain and then the storm. In the Mariner's dream, which comes in the first heaven-sent sleep, we have the presentiment of the rain and storm, a dream which corresponds to the dream of the Polar Spirit which had hinted to the fellow mariners the nature of the crime: in both cases, at this instinctive, subrational level, the truth is darkly shadowed forth before it is realized in the waking world. In the Mariner's dream, before the real rain comes, the "silly buckets" are filled with dew. Upon waking and drinking the rain, the Mariner, in his light and blessed condition, hears a roaring wind; then, as the Gloss puts it, there are "strange sights and commotions in the sky and the elements," presided over by the moon, which hangs at the edge of the black cloud. The moon of imagination and the storm of creative vitality here join triumphantly to celebrate the Mariner's salvation.

But here let us pause to observe a peculiar fact. The wind does not reach the ship, and the Polar Spirit, who had originally set forth on an errand of vengeance, provides the power of locomotion for the ship. Though he has been functioning as the sinister aspect of the imagination, he, too, is now drawn, in "obedience to the angelic troop," into the new beneficent activity. Not that he is to lose entirely his sinister aspect; we shall see that his vengeance persists, for the Mariner, in his role as the *poète maudit,* will show that the imagination is a curse as well as a blessing. But for the moment, though grudgingly, the Spirit joins the forces of salvation.

What now, we may ask, is the logic of this situation? If the wind were to drive the ship, the action would not be adapted to show the role of the Polar Spirit. Furthermore, if the wind were to drive the ship, the fusion of the natural and the supernatural in the terrible and festal activity below and above the sea would not be exhibited. And this is important, for here we have another moment of fusion of the primary and secondary themes: wind, moon, and Polar Spirit belong to the secondary theme of the imagination, but the "angelic troop," in obedience to which the Spirit acts, belongs properly to the primary theme, the theme of the "One Life" and the sacramental vision.

I have said that the angelic troop here serves to introduce the primary theme into the episode. Certainly, in the reanimation of the bodies of the fellow mariners, there is implicit the idea of regeneration and resurrection, and in this way the participation in the general meaning of the episode becomes clear. But the behavior of the re-inspirited bodies, taken in itself, offers a difficulty. Taken at the natural level, the manipulating of the sails and ropes serves no purpose. Taken at the symbolic level, this activity is activity without content, a "lag" in the poem, a "meaningless marvel." And the spirits in the bodies give us an added difficulty. When day comes, they desert the bodies and as sweet sounds dart to the sun. The sun, under whose aegis the bad events of the poem occur, here appears in a "good" association.

Our problem of interpreting these "good" associations is parallel to that of dealing with the moon when it appears in "bad" association. I shall treat it analogously, by looking at it in the special context and not in isolation. This redemption of the sun—for we may call it that—comes as part of the general rejoicing when the proper order has been re-established in the universe. The "understanding," shall we say, no longer exists in abstraction, no longer partakes of death, but has its proper role in the texture of things and partakes of the general blessedness. It is, for the moment, "spiritualized." I say for the moment, for at noon, the hour when the sun is in its highest power and is most likely to assert itself in "abstraction," the sun resumes briefly its inimical role and prevents the happy forward motion of the ship:

> The Sun, right up above the mast,
> Had fixed her to the ocean.

As the Gloss explains here, this event takes place when the Polar Spirit, after having obediently conveyed the ship to the Line, still "requireth vengeance." In other words, the inimical force of the sun is felt at the moment when the power of imagination seems to be turning away vengefully from the Mariner. But this crisis is passed, for after all the Mariner has been redeemed, and the ship plunges forward again with such suddenness that the Mariner is thrown into a "swound."

In his swound the Mariner receives a fuller revelation of his situation and of the nature of the forces operating about him. He learns these things, it is important to notice, in the dream—just as the fellow mariners had received the first intimation of the presence of the Polar Spirit through dreams. And the significance of this fact is the same: the dream is not at the level of the "understanding," but is the appropriate mode by which the special kind of knowledge of the imagination should be revealed.

It is in this dream that the Mariner for the first time receives an explicit statement of the relation of the Albatross and the Polar Spirit. Meanwhile the Gloss tells us that the Polar Spirit, having been assured that the Mariner will continue to do penance (as the Mariner himself learns from the Second Voice), returns southward. But the ship, which had been propelled by the Polar Spirit, continues on its way by another means, as the Second Voice describes. Do we have here an "unmeaning marvel," or is there some content to this business? An interpretation at this point probably demands more forcing than at any other, but there is, perhaps, a possible one consistent with the rest of the poem. The angelic troop and the Polar Spirit (the first associated with the primary theme, the second with the secondary theme) are both "supernatural"—as the Gloss somewhat superfluously remarks. But the Second Voice gives the Mariner, and us, a scientific, i.e., "natural," explanation of the progress of the ship. So we have here the supernatural powers (of the two orders) acting by the agency of the natural mechanism of the world—the supernatural and the natural conspiring together on the Mariner's behalf after his redemption.

There is, however, an additional item to be considered in the vision, the description of the moon and the ocean given by the Second Voice:

> 'Still as a slave before his lord,
> The ocean hath no blast;
> His great bright eye most silently
> Up to the Moon is cast—
>
> If he may know which way to go;
> For she guides him smooth or grim.
> See, brother, see! how graciously
> She looketh down on him.'

This is a fairly obvious definition of the role of the moon—the adored, the guiding, the presiding power.

After this definition in dream of the role of the moon, the Mariner wakes to find it shining and the dead men standing about with their moonstruck eyes fixing a curse upon him. This scene recalls two previous scenes of the poem. First, it recalls the other scene of the curse by the eye in moonlight before the redemption of the Mariner. Second, it recalls the main redemption scene when the Mariner blesses the snakes in the moonlight. With the first we have here a parallelism developing a contrast, and with the second a parallelism developing a repetition. For in this, we have a second redemption scene—the relief from the curse, which, the Gloss says, is "finally expiated." But as the spell is snapped, there is a moment in which the Mariner is fearfully bemused like one who knows

> . . . a frightful fiend
> Doth close behind him tread.

This last hint of the curse disappears with the rising of the strange breeze. It is not a "natural" breeze, for it does not ripple the water—it blows only upon the Mariner. The ship moves, but not by the breeze (presumably by the angelic troop, as before). It is the creative wind again, blowing only upon the Mariner, fanning his cheek, but also mingling "strangely" with his "fears"—a hint of the ambiguous power of the imagination. The rising of the breeze now, after this second redemption scene, corresponds to the rising of the great storm after the first redemption scene—a storm which, we must remember, was both terrible and festal in its aspect. The rising of the breeze now also recalls the first storm which drove the ship south in Part I —a parallelism by contrast, for the first storm was all "enemy" while the present breeze, though it mingles strangely with the Mariner's fears, is a sweet breeze.

Suddenly, under the sweet breeze, the Mariner descries the home port. Appropriately, it is drenched in the magnificent moonlight. But now we are to have another kind of light, too. By every corpse on deck stands a seraph-man with a body all of light as a signal to the land. So here, in the two kinds of light by which the return is accomplished, the men of light (associated with the primary theme) and the moon (associated with the secondary theme), we have a final fusion of the imagination and the sacramental vision. We may, as it were, take them to be aspects of the same reality.

This fusion, with the beginning of Part VII, is restated by means of the figure of the Hermit, who is both priest of God and priest of Nature. We may look at the matter in this way: The theme of the "One Life," of the sacramental vision, is essentially religious—it presents us with the world, as the crew of the ship are presented with the Albatross, in "God's name." As we have seen, the poem is shot through with religious associations. On the other hand, the theme of imagination is essentially aesthetic—it presents us with the "great forms" of nature, but those forms as actively seized upon by human mind and loved *not merely as vehicles for transcendental meaning but in themselves as participating in the reality which they "render intelligible."* The theme is essentially aesthetic, but it is also "natural" in the sense just defined as contrasted with the sense in which nature is regarded as the neutral material worked on by the mere "understanding." The Hermit, who kneels in the woods, embodies both views, both themes.

The Hermit, however, has another aspect. He is also the priest of Society, for it is by the Hermit, who urges the Pilot on despite his fears, that the Mariner is received back into the world of men. This rejoining of the world of men is not, we observe, accomplished simply by the welcoming committee. There is the terrific sound which sinks the ship and flings the stunned Mariner into the Pilot's boat. In the logic of the symbolic structure this would be, I presume, a repetition of the wind or storm motif: the creative storm has a part in re-establishing the Mariner's relation to other men. Even if the destruction of the ship is regarded, as some readers regard it, as a final act of the Polar Spirit, to show, as it were, what he could do if he had a mind to, the symbolic import is not altered, for the Spirit belongs to the cluster of imagination which has the terrifying and cataclysmic as well as benign aspect. As a matter of fact, since the Gloss has earlier dismissed the Polar Spirit at the end of Part V, saying that he "returneth southward," it seems more reasonable to me to interpret the destruction of the ship as the work of the angelic troop, whose capacity to work marvels has already been amply demonstrated. And this reading gives us a fuller symbolic burden, too, and is consistent with the final fusion of themes which we observe in this general episode. At the level of the primary theme, the angelic troop wipe out the crime (i.e., the "criminal" ship and the dead bodies); at the level of the secondary theme, they do so by means of the "storm," which belongs to the symbolic cluster of the imagination.

Part V

By this reading of the poem the central and crucial fact is the fusion of the primary and secondary themes. And this means that the poem suddenly takes its place as a document of the very central and crucial issue of the period: the problem of truth and poetry. I do not mean to imply that this problem was first recognized by the Romantics. It had had a statement at least as early as the Platonic dialogue *Ion*. But with the English Romantics it was not only a constant topic for criticism, but was, directly or indirectly, an obsessive theme for poetry itself. . . .

The fusion of the theme of the "One Life" and the theme of imagination is the expression in the poem of Coleridge's general belief concerning the relation of truth and poetry, of morality and beauty. We find at the very turning point of the poem, the moment of the blessing of the water snakes, an explicit presentation of the idea. The sequence of events gives us, first, a recognition of the happiness of the water snakes in their fulfillment of being—they participate in the serene order of the universe. Like the stars and the moon which move unperturbed on their appointed business while the Mariner is fixed in his despair, the snakes, which appear, too, as light-giving, participate in the universal fullness of being. Seeing them thus, the Mariner can exclaim:

> O happy living things!

After this utterance, we have the recognition of the beauty of the water snakes under the aegis of the moon—that recognition being determined, we have seen, by the recognition of their place in the universal pattern:

> . . . no tongue
> Their beauty might declare:

Then love gushes from the Mariner's heart, the response at the level of instinctive feeling. Then he blesses them; that is, the instinctive feeling stirred by the recognition of beauty, finds its formal and objective expression. But he blesses them "unawares," and the word may be important, corresponding in this little account of the natural history of a "poem" or blessing, composed by the Mariner, to Wordsworth's word *spontaneous* in his phrase "the spontaneous overflow of powerful feelings" and Coleridge's word *unconscious* in the statement, in "On Poesy," that "There is in genius an unconscious activity; nay, that is the genius in the man of genius." So we may have here, and I do not mean this too whimsically, the case of a man who saves his own soul by composing a poem. But what Coleridge actually means is, of course, that the writing of a poem is simply a specialized example of a general process which leads to salvation. After the Mariner has composed his poem of blessing, he can begin the long voyage home.

He gets home, in the moonlight, which, we recall, is the light of imagination, and in the end he celebrates the chain of love which binds human society together, and the universe. But even here the

Hermit, who officially reintroduces him into human society, is a priest of Nature as well as a priest of God; and the relation between man and Nature is established by the imagination, and so the Hermit is also a priest of imagination. In other words, imagination not only puts man in tune with other men, with society: it provides the great discipline of sympathy. The socializing function of the imagination was never lost sight of by the Romantics. The poet is the man speaking of men, Wordsworth declares, and Shelley says in the *Defence*: "The great instrument of moral good is the imagination," for it leads man to "put himself in the place of another and of many others," so that "the pains and pleasures of his species must become his own." Over and over again in that generation we encounter the idea, and the Mariner returns to proclaim how sweet it is to walk "with a goodly company."

If the Mariner returns to celebrate the chain of love which binds human society and the universe, the fact should remind us that the occasion is a wedding and his audience a wedding guest. But it is sometimes argued that the Mariner repudiates marriage, contrasting it with the religious devotion indulged in "with a goodly company." Now the contrast is certainly in the poem, and is involved in one of the personal themes. But in the total poem we cannot take the fact of the contrast as being unqualified. At the level of doctrine, we do not have contrast between marriage and sacramental love, but one as image of the other. It is no accident that the Mariner stops a light-hearted reveler on the way to a marriage feast. What he tells the wedding guest is that the human love, which the guest presumably takes to be an occasion for merriment, must be understood in the context of universal love and that only in such a context may it achieve its meaning. The end of the poem gives a dramatic scaling of the love, in lines 591–609.

> What loud uproar bursts from that door!
> The wedding-guests are there:
> But in the garden-bower the bride
> And bride-maids singing are:
> And hark the little vesper bell,
> Which biddeth me to prayer!
>
> O Wedding-Guest! this soul hath been
> Alone on a wide wide sea: . . .
>
> O sweeter than the marriage-feast,
> 'Tis sweeter far to me,
> To walk together to the kirk
> With a goodly company!—

The scale starts with the rude merriment, uninstructed and instinctive. Then the next phase, introduced by the significant word *but,* gives us the bride in the garden singing with the bridesmaids, retired from the general din and giving us, presumably, a kind of secular hymn of love. Then comes the vesper bell calling to prayer. The significance of the prayer is immediately indicated by the sudden statement that the Mariner's soul—and the use of the word *soul* here is important—has been alone on a wide sea: the Mariner now sees the chain of love which gives meaning to the marriage feast. In one of its aspects the poem is a prothalamion.

But we must ask ourselves more narrowly about the Mariner's situation, even as he proclaims his message of love. He is, we recall, a wanderer, with some shadow hanging over him of those two great wanderers, the Jew and Cain. His situation is paradoxical. Now from one point of view it is proper that the prophet of universal charity, even though he celebrates the village life of the goodly company walking to church together, should himself have no fixed address, for that would in a way deprive his message, symbolically at least, of its universality. But his wandering is not only a mark of his blessed vision: it is also a curse. So we have here a peculiar and paradoxical situation: the poem is a poem in which the poetic imagination appears in a regenerative and healing capacity, but in the end the hero, who has, presumably, been healed, appears in one of his guises as the *poète maudit.* So we learn that the imagination does not only bless, for even as it blesses it lays on a curse. Though the Mariner brings the word which is salvation, he cannot quite save himself and taste the full joy of the fellowship he advertises. Society looks askance at him. When he first returns home and is flung into the Pilot's boat (significantly by the creative storm), the ordinary mortals there are appalled: the Pilot falls down in a fit; the Pilot's boy "doth crazy go" and declares flatly that the Mariner is the devil himself; and even the Hermit has to conquer his mortal trepidations in prayer (though the priest ought to understand the artist as another person dedicated to ideal values). And even now, long after, the Wedding Guest has moments of terror under the glittering eye. The very gifts, the hypnotic eye, the "strange power of speech," set the Mariner apart.

Now, as we look back over the poem, we may see that this doubtful doubleness of the imagination has more than once been apparent. Creativity is a wind, a storm, which is sometimes inimical (as in the first storm in Part I) and is sometimes saving (as after the blessing of the snakes). But even in its most gentle manifestation, as the light breeze blows sweetly on the Mariner's brow on the voyage home, it "mingles strangely" with his "fears." There is always a strain of terror with the beauty, and in the end it is a shattering, supernatural blast which sinks the ship and delivers the Mariner to the waters of the home port even as the beneficent moon looks down.

The Mariner will be rescued and will pass like night from land to land. Let us linger on this phrase: like night. For even this tells us something. It gives us first the effortless, universal sweep, a sense of the universality of the Mariner's message which is carried from land to land. It tells us, too, by the easy, conventional equation of *dark* and *accursed* that the Mariner is the *poète maudit*. But night in this poem has a special body of associations, and with night we may have here, as a result of the long accumulation of night scenes, always with the association of the moon, a hint of the healing role of the imagination—a beneficent countering to the burden of the curse which is carried in the phrase. The phrase, in its special context, repeats, in little, the paradoxical situation of the Mariner.

Earlier I have said that we find in the blessing of the snakes a little fable of the creative process—the natural history of a poem of blessing. But in the end of the poem we have another fable of the creative process, and perhaps a fuller statement of Coleridge's conception of the poet, the man with the power which comes unbidden and which is an "agony" until it finds words, the power which wells up from the unconscious but which is the result of a moral experience and in its product, the poem, the "tale" told by the Mariner, will "teach"—for that is the word the Mariner uses. It is a paradoxical process. . . .

Part VI

I have tried to show, by dwelling on details as well as on the broad, central images, that there is in *The Ancient Mariner* a relatively high degree of expressive integration. There may be lags and lapses in fulfilling the basic creative idea, but, according to my reading, these lags and lapses are minor. But one school of thought has always held that the lags and lapses are far from minor, that there is no pervasive logic in the poem. Wordsworth, of course, said as much, as did Mrs. Barbauld with her complaint of improbability, and Southey in his review of the piece in *The Critical Review*. Even Lamb, in defending the poem against Southey and declaring it to have the true power of playing "tricks with the mind," was constrained to admit that parts of the poem were "fertile in unmeaning miracles." And later, in defending the poem against Wordsworth's charge that it was not integrated, he again admitted that he disliked "all the miraculous parts of it."

We must remember that the poem to which all of the critics referred was not the poem as it stands before us today. I do not argue that it would have made any difference to Mrs. Barbauld, or even to Wordsworth, but Coleridge did arrive at, by the time of the publication in *Sibylline Leaves* (1817), two major changes: he added the Gloss, which should have made the structure of the poem clearer, and he revised the text. Whether or not Coleridge was led to these changes by the criticism of the obscurity and lack of logic, the revision of the text itself was in accordance with his own theory of composition, that the parts of a work should participate in the expressiveness of the whole. So we have, in the important omissions made in the last version, a purging of at least most of the "unmeaning miracles" of which Lamb presumably complained, the descriptions of Death on the specter-bark and of the burning arms of the spirits at the time of the homecoming. . . .

Coleridge was aware of the attacks on the poem on the grounds of the improbability caused by the use of the supernatural, and when he came to the final revision he gave us, it would seem, his answer. It is in the long motto by Burnet, which calls special attention to the supernatural element in the poem. "I readily believe," Burnet says, "that in the universe are more invisible beings than visible." He continues:

> But who will expound to us the nature of them all, and their ranks and relationships and distinguishing characteristics and the functions of each? What is it they perform? What regions do they inhabit? Ever about the knowledge of these things circles the thought of man, never reaching it. Meanwhile, it is pleasant, I must confess, sometimes to contemplate in the mind, as in a picture, the image of this greater and better world: that the mind, accustomed to the little things of daily life, may not be narrowed overmuch and lose itself in trivial reflections. But meanwhile must we diligently seek after truth, maintaining just measure, that we may distinguish things certain from uncertain, day from night.

It is worthy of note that this motto was added in the edition of 1817, long after the heyday of the first enthusiastic speculations on the Quantock Hills and now in the cold calculation of a critical middle age bent upon making the masterpiece more comprehensible. I have already indicated how the last sentence of the motto points to the night-day, moon-sun opposition in the poem, and ties with that basic symbol; and I take the use of the motto to be not a piece of whimsical mumbo-jumbo or a vain parade of learning, but a device for pointing at a central fact of the poem. It says that the world is full of powers and presences not visible to the physical eye (or by the "understanding"): this is a way of saying that there is a spiritual order of universal love, the sacramental vision, and of imagination; that nature, if understood aright—that is, by the imagination—offers us vital meanings. It is simply a way of underscoring the function of the supernatural machinery and atmosphere in the poem, a way of saying that it participates in the symbolic tissue of the poem.

For I take the poem to be one in which the vital integration is of a high order, not one of the "great, formless poems" which the Romantics are accused of writing, and not a poem which would fit into T. S. Eliot's formula of the dissociated sensibility of the period. I take it to be a poem central and seminal for the poet himself. Though a philosopher has said that "it would be pedantry to look for philosophical doctrines" in these magical lines, and though a literary scholar finds here "merely the aroma, the fine flavor," of the poet's meditations, if we do look closely at the magical lines and look at them in the light of the poet's lifelong preoccupations, we may come to conclude, with Leslie Stephen, that "the germ of all Coleridge's utterances may be found . . . in the 'Ancient Mariner.' " It is central for Coleridge, but it is also central for its age, providing, not a comment on an age, but a focus of the being and issues of that age. It is, in short, a work of "pure imagination." . . .

Part VII

One last word: In this essay I have not attempted to "explain" how poetry appeals, or why. I have been primarily concerned to give a discursive reading of the symbol which is the poem, in so far as I can project the import of the symbol in such a fashion. I humbly trust that I am not more insensitive than most to the "magical lines," but at the same time I cannot admit that our experience, even our aesthetic experience, is ineluctably and vindictively divided into the "magical" and the rational, with an abyss between. If poetry does anything for us, it reconciles, by its symbolical reading of experience (for by its very nature it is in itself a myth of the unity of being), the self-divisive internecine malices which arise at the superficial level on which we conduct most of our living.

And *The Ancient Mariner* is a poem on this subject.

"The Ancient Mariner"

by Humphry House

I quoted in Chapter I, as an example of Coleridge's public prose style, the opening of the Prefatory Note to "The Wanderings of Cain"; it describes how that curious prose fragment came into being and it ends by saying that the whole scheme for the collaboration with Wordsworth in a poem about Cain "broke up in a laugh: and the Ancient Mariner was written instead." This is only one among a number of partial records left by Coleridge himself, or by the Wordsworths, of the origin of the "Mariner." These different records piece together into a quite intelligible and consistent account, too familiar to repeat.[1] But "The Wanderings of Cain" has a special place in that account because it shows how the subject of terrible guilt, suffering, expiation and wandering was already in Coleridge's mind before the various hints which were to form the outline of the Mariner's story came together. Cain's "countenance told in a strange and terrible language of agonies that had been, and were still to continue to be." These agonies were related to a landscape in tune with them:

> The scene around was desolate; as far as the eye could reach it was desolate: the bare rocks faced each other, and left a long and wide interval of thin white sand.[2]

It is even verbally but a few steps to "the wide wide sea."

In another draft fragment of the Cain poem[3] a rather obscure and evasive sentence says that God inflicted punishment on Cain "because he neglected to make a proper use of his senses, etc." Later in this draft come alligators and tigers in close conjunction, just as they occurred together in a speech of the Wandering Jew in Lewis's *The*

"The Ancient Mariner" by Humphry House. From Coleridge: The Clark Lectures, *1951–1952 (London: Rupert Hart-Davis, Ltd., 1953), pp. 84–113. Reprinted by permission of the publisher.*

[1] The other leading references are conveniently given in Lowes, pp. 222–24, 528–31. Cf. *BL* [*Biographia Literaria*, ed. J. Shawcross (London, 1907)], Ch. xiv.

[2] *PW* [*The Complete Poetical Works of Samuel Taylor Coleridge,* ed. E. H. Coleridge (Oxford, 1912)], I, 289, ll. 67–72.

[3] *PW*, pp. 285–6, n. 1.

Monk, which Coleridge reviewed in *The Critical Review* for February 1797.[4] The Mariner bears traces of both these two traditional figures, Cain and the Wandering Jew.[5]

Not only once, but twice, Coleridge and Wordsworth began to collaborate in an exceedingly light-hearted way in works which dealt with crime, guilt, expiation and wandering. If we are broadly able to trust Coleridge's account, "The Wanderings of Cain" was begun as a composition-race: and there is no reason at all to doubt that "The Ancient Mariner" was begun by them jointly to raise £5 to pay the expenses of a walking-tour. It was thus an entirely unexpected by-product of Coleridge's main poetical plans. Those plans were, as we saw from the letter to Cottle which I quoted in the last chapter, of Miltonic size and seriousness. There is evidence, as Professor R. C. Bald has shown,[6] for believing that he was deliberately reading with the idea of writing two main works, a series of Hymns to the Sun, Moon and Elements, and an Epic on the Origin of Evil. It is hardly necessary even to say how much matter in the "Mariner" overlaps with what might have gone into those two works.

We may even suggest that the accident, so to speak, of beginning the "Mariner" on that November evening in 1797 released Coleridge from some of the burden of his Miltonic responsibilities and helped to split his ambitious synthesising aim of bringing all human knowledge together in the frame of one or more huge poems. I have already tried to show how, in the more ambitious poems just before this period, he was attempting, without much success, to synthesise politics, religion and philosophy in a highly Miltonic style. Now the aims and material split. It has been observed by Dr. Tillyard how very unpolitical "The Ancient Mariner" is. "Frost at Midnight" (dated February 1798—that is while the "Mariner" was still being written) is, if possible, less political still. It is interesting that Coleridge's best political poem, "France: an Ode," is also dated February 1798: creative energy used in one direction and style seems also to have released it in other directions and styles. A political Ode in the Gray/Mason tradition, and a blank-verse meditative poem, soaring right away from its origins in Cowper, were written in among work on the "Mariner," which differed from both. There could be no clearer disproof of the narrowness of Coleridge's poetic range than the fact that these three poems are contemporary.

[4] This review is reprinted in *CMC* [*Coleridge's Miscellaneous Criticism,* ed. T. M. Raysor (London, 1936)], 370–78.

[5] For fuller details see Lowes, pp. 243–60.

[6] Bald [R. C. Bald, "*Coleridge and The Ancient Mariner:* Addenda to *The Road to Xanadu,*" *Nineteenth Century Studies* (Cornell, 1940)], pp. 15 ff.

Little need be said about the context of styles to which the "Mariner" belongs: it has plain affiliations with Gothic horrors, of which Lewis was the fashionable exponent; and it is noticeable too that in the original volume of the *Lyrical Ballads* "The Ancient Mariner" is the only poem which derives its style from the traditional ballads as they were then available in Percy, rather than from the later ballad of broadsheet.[7] The precision, success and care, with which Coleridge later cut out many of the cruder traces of these origins—the pseudo-antique spelling, the more glaring archaisms of vocabulary, some of the marvels—is fresh evidence of the justice of his detailed judgement: but yet, when all these changes had been made, it is still remarkable how many features of ballad idiom and method the poem still retains and completely assimilates, diverting and modifying them to its own particular effects. It is partly by these means that the poem manages to escape history and yet retain tradition. Though it will not tie to a table of dates or a map, the "Mariner" yet uses the keepings of European tradition and all the details of wind and weather which every map implies. Its imagery, both of religion and of the elements, goes deep below the surface of what we may happen to remember or happen to have seen.

But at the same time it uses to the full the vividness of visual description which was one of Coleridge's great poetic strengths. A friend of mine recently said he could not read Coleridge any more—no, not even "The Ancient Mariner": he could not stand all the supernatural part; but only a few sentences later he went on to say that on a slow sea-voyage to Africa he got up early and walked round the deck reciting the poem to himself, and that nothing could have better fitted his mood or described what he saw than

> The fair breeze blew, the white foam flew,
> The furrow followed free.[8]

Scarcely any reader, from first acquaintance in childhood, has not felt that the first, most elementary contact with the poem leaves such isolated descriptions fixed in the memory, and it is only a step further, if it is a step at all, to feel, at the next level of relevance, the perfect attunement between the descriptions and the states of the Mariner's mind.

[7] See the Percy version of "The Wandering Jew"; "Sir Cauline" for some of the vocabulary; "Young Waters" and "King Estmere" especially for past tenses with "did." William Taylor's translation of Bürger's "Lenore" must not be forgotten.

[8] ll. 103–4; all quotations from the "Mariner" are from the text in *PW*, I, 187–209.

> Down dropt the breeze, the sails dropt down,
> 'Twas sad as sad could be;
> And we did speak only to break
> The silence of the sea! [9]

None of Coleridge's poems shows more completely developed in practice the principle of description which was quoted earlier from his letter to Sotheby of 1802:

> Never to see or describe any interesting appearance in nature without connecting it, by dim analogies, with the moral world proves faintness of impression. Nature has her proper interest, and he will know what it is who believes and feels that everything has a life of its own, and that we are all *One Life*. A poet's heart and intellect should be *combined*, intimately combined and unified with the great appearances of nature and not merely held in solution and loose mixture with them, in the shape of formal similes.[10]

The full relevance of this to "The Ancient Mariner" will begin to appear gradually in what I have to say later. The present relevance is that in the poem the method of relating nature to the moral world is not by "dim analogies," nor "in the shape of formal similes" (there arc very few), but by the poet's heart and intellect being intimately *combined* and unified with the great appearances of nature. The method of conjunction is immediate in the natural imagery, and it is only by understanding the imagery that the "moral world" can be understood. For the present a single simple instance must be enough.

> And now there came both mist and snow,
> And it grew wondrous cold:
> And ice, mast-high, came floating by,
> As green as emerald.

> And through the drifts the snowy clifts
> Did send a dismal sheen:
> Nor shapes of men nor beasts we ken—
> The ice was all between.

> The ice was here, the ice was there,
> The ice was all around:
> It cracked and growled, and roared and howled,
> Like noises in a swound! [11]

[9] ll. 107–10.
[10] *L* [Letters of Samuel Taylor Coleridge (London, 1895)], I, 403–4.
[11] ll. 51–62.

In those stanzas it is *in* the descriptive phrases "As green as emerald" and "a dismal sheen" that the double mood of admiration and fear is conveyed: and the double character of this mood is important.

"The great appearances of nature" play an overwhelming part in the poem, and their part was emphasised and further explained in the prose gloss that was added in 1817. Lowes put this side of the poem epigrammatically by saying that the chief characters in "The Ancient Mariner" are "Earth, Air, Fire and Water." [12] By chief "characters" we must understand also chief channels of action—for it is through the elements that the Mariner is acted upon.

The function of the elements and heavenly bodies is not merely to *image* the Mariner's spiritual states (though indeed they do this), but also to provide in the narrative structure of the poem the link between the Mariner as ordinary man, and the Mariner as one acquainted with the invisible world, which has its own sets of values.

This link is first suggested in the idea that the Albatross has a power of control over the elements: it is continued in the idea of the plaguing spirit that followed the ship nine fathoms deep from the land of mist and snow. The skeleton ship with the figures of Death and Life-in-Death is linked to the phenomena of the tropical sunset:

> The Sun's rim dips; the stars rush out:
> At one stride comes the dark;
> With far-heard whisper, o'er the sea,
> Off shot the spectre bark.[13]

The angelic spirits who inspire the dead men to work the ship are sent to release the ship from the control of the daemons of the elements; and the spirit from the South Pole works under their orders. The two voices in Parts V and VI are two fellow daemons of the Polar Spirit, two "invisible inhabitants of the element," as the gloss calls them. And finally the ship is brought back to port under the undisputed control of angelic spirits, but accompanied by a wind.

Across this whole system of daemons of the elements and angelic spirits lies the framework of ordinary Catholic theology—Christ and Mary Queen of Heaven, and in the ending the ordinary Catholic practices of confession, absolution and church-going.

The inter-relation of the different spiritual beings is one of the hardest points in the poem to be clear or confident about; and it is best, approaching the more doubtful through the less, to begin by discussing the poem's more obvious bearings on the "moral world,"

[12] Lowes, pp. 74 ff.
[13] ll. 199–202.

and indeed to establish first that it has a bearing on the moral world at all. For even this has sometimes been disputed. We must start from Coleridge's one main comment on the poem, as it is reported in the *Table Talk* under 31 May 1830:

> Mrs. Barbauld once told me that she admired the Ancient Mariner very much, but that there were two faults in it,—it was improbable, and had no moral. As for the probability, I owned that that might admit some question; but as to the want of a moral, I told her that in my own judgment the poem had too much; and that the only, or chief fault, if I might say so, was the obtrusion of the moral sentiment so openly on the reader as a principle or cause of action in a work of such pure imagination. It ought to have had no more moral than the Arabian Nights' tale of the merchant's sitting down to eat dates by the side of a well, and throwing the shells aside, and lo! a genie starts up, and says he *must* kill the aforesaid merchant *because* one of the date shells had, it seems, put out the eye of the genie's son.

The story of the Merchant and the Genie in *The Arabian Nights* is briefly this. A merchant is travelling in a desert with nothing to eat but some biscuits and dates in a wallet. He sits down to eat dates and throws the stones about: a huge and terrible genie appears, with a great scimitar, and says he will cut off the merchant's head. Why? Because one of the stones was flung into the eye of the genie's son and killed him. The merchant pleads that it was quite accidental: but the genie is relentless. Finally the genie allows the merchant one year's respite. He is free to go home to provide for his wife and children, and to order his affairs. This he does, with great justice and generosity and, after a struggle, he returns to the same spot in the desert, as arranged with the genie, exactly one year later. Here he falls in with three old men, mysterious strangers, to whom he tells his story; the genie then appears again. And each of the strangers in turn makes a bargain with the genie that if he can tell the genie a story more marvellous than he has ever heard before, the genie is to remit one-third of the merchant's punishment. The stories cap each other for marvellousness; the genie is honest to the bargain; the merchant goes free and triumphant home, and the three old men go off mysteriously into the desert as they came.

Now this story has not got a "moral" in the sense that there is a clear explicit detachable maxim which neatly sums up the didactic drift of it. But it seems equally clear that one cannot possibly read the story without being very aware of moral issues in it; aware that its whole development is governed by moral situations, and that without them there wouldn't really be a story. The arbitrariness of the genie; the awful consequences to the merchant of what was originally, on his side, a pure accident; the thoughts of the merchant for his family; these are moral matters. The generosity and exactness with which he arranged his affairs in the year of respite is developed very fully in the story: and much is made of the struggle about his bargain to return, and of the punctuality and faithfulness with which he kept it. It is very difficult indeed, in reading the story, not to see in his final release, as the result of the three old men's tales, a reward for his honourableness and care in all his dealings. And when one has got so far, it is not difficult to see that—always allowing for the fact that no "maxim" conveys the *whole* moral of a story—some such maxim as this, deduced from it, is not irrelevant: "The arbitrary character of fate may be overcome by human honour and goodness; and there may be mysterious powers in the world which aid these virtues." In the *Arabian Nights* version this moral, or anything like it, is not in Coleridge's words "obtruded too openly." But to deny altogether that it (or something like it) is there (when the whole story depends on the genie's arbitrariness, the merchant's honourableness and his final release) would seem to me a grotesque example of wilful blindness.

We do not know how well Coleridge remembered the story or how accurately his nephew reported what he said. But as the *Table Talk* passage stands, it is surely clear that Coleridge never said or meant that the "Mariner" neither had nor was meant to have a moral bearing or a "moral sentiment." He said the fault was *"the obtrusion of the* moral sentiment *so openly* . . . in a work of such pure imagination." And this seems to point to his possible dissatisfaction with the summary of the "moral" as a kind of didactic epigram towards the end:

> He prayeth well, who loveth well
> Both man and bird and beast.

> He prayeth best, who loveth best
> All things both great and small;
> For the dear God who loveth us,
> He made and loveth all.[14]

It is obvious that those lines do rub the point home and that they may, when detached from their context, be degraded to the status of a motto in "almanac art," or used to express the quite worthy desire to put out crumbs for the dicky-birds on a cold and frosty morning. But coming in context, after the richness and terror of the poem, it is no more a banal moral apothegm, but a moral which has its meaning *because it has been lived.*

All recent full discussions of "The Ancient Mariner" have taken this for granted. In what follows I owe a great deal to three such discus-

[14] ll. 612–17.

sions, one by Dr. Tillyard;[15] one by Dr. Bowra;[16] and one by the American writer and critic Mr. Robert Penn Warren.[17] All agree, however much they differ from each other, that the poem has a very serious moral and spiritual bearing on human life: and they are surely right. For Coleridge, talking in 1830, could not possibly have meant to exclude all moral relevance from the working of the "pure imagination" when his whole developed critical theory stressed again and again the union of heart and head, the special power of the poet to bring "the whole soul of man into activity." [18]

Coleridge has set us a special problem of critical method. It is obvious that his own creative experience must have deeply affected his critical theories and practice: but he never fully brought the two into relation; he rarely adduced his own poems as instances, and never expounded them. Furthermore, his important critical work was all a good deal later than most of his important creative work. We cannot thus be sure how much of his critical opinion may fairly be carried back into 1797-8 and brought to bear on his own greatest poetry. It is very hard to be fair, and not to pick out what suits us and reject the rest. It is, for instance, tempting to use Coleridge's later distinctions between allegory and symbol in interpreting "The Ancient Mariner"; but they had not been expressed in 1797-8. In fact, we may be misled if we start the critique of the "Mariner" and "Kubla Khan" with this disjunction of allegory from symbol in mind. For all allegory involves symbolism, and in proportion as symbolism becomes developed and coherent it tends towards allegory. This is one of the problems involved in Mr. Warren's exciting essay: he starts as a "symbolist" criticising all the "allegorisers" and ends up in something so organised and precise that Coleridge, anyway, would probably have called it an allegorisation. But Mr. Warren would be quite willing to accept that, provided only that his kind of allegory is seen to be distinct from simple "two-dimensional" allegory.

The poem's very richness at once tempts and defeats definiteness of interpretation; as we commit ourselves to the development of one strand of meaning we find that in the very act of doing so we are excluding something else of importance.

An example of this difficulty occurs on the threshold of interpretation, in the opinion we form about the Mariner's relation to ordinary human beings and the relation of the voyage to ordinary human life.

[15] E. M. W. Tillyard, *Five Poems*, pp. 66–86.
[16] C. M. Bowra, *The Romantic Imagination*, Ch. iii.
[17] *The Rime of the Ancient Mariner*, with an essay by Robert Penn Warren (New York: Reynal and Hitchcock, 1946). [See this volume, pp. 21–47.]
[18] *BL*, II, 12.

Dr. Tillyard, struck (as everybody must be struck) by the similarities in spirit between the poem and the seventeenth-century voyages—

> We were the first that ever burst
> Into that silent sea—

as voyages of adventure and discovery, and using, to support his argument, the later Coleridge passage in the *Biographia* about the range of hills which must be crossed by an inquiring spirit, maintains that the Mariner himself is a mental and spiritual adventurer, "an unusually enquiring spirit," that he together with the rest of the crew are, from the accepted social point of view, *self-appointed* outcasts and criminals; and that the sea-voyage indicates "spiritual adventure" which they go out of their way to seek.[19]

But how is this present in the poem? The beginning of the Mariner's own account of the voyage contains no hint that he thought of the voyage as a high spiritual enterprise at variance with current limited social ideas, a conscious seeking of adventure. The ship starts off in an atmosphere of communal agreement and pleasure:

> The ship was cheered, the harbour cleared,
> Merrily did we drop
> Below the kirk, below the hill,
> Below the lighthouse top.[20]

The voyage, it seems, began normally, commonly, happily, the crew at one both with the society they left and with each other. In the literature of sea-going the antecedents are rather to be found in such voyages as that described by Herodotus—certainly used by Coleridge when he wrote

> The Sun now rose upon the right—[21]

the voyage in which the Phoenician seamen doubled the Cape without knowing that there was a Cape.[22] Adventure came upon them unaware.

The Mariner, said Wordsworth in rude complaint, "does not act, but is continually acted upon." There is, surely, an important element of truth in this, though it does not in the least derogate from the

---

[19] *Five Poems*, pp. 70–71.
[20] ll. 21–4.
[21] l. 83.
[22] Hdt. IV, 42, 3–4. Coleridge would certainly have known the passage in the original, and also, as Lowes shows (p. 127), the quotation and application of it in Bryan Edwards's *History . . . of the British Colonies in the West Indies.*

poem's merits.[23] There are only three points in the poem at which the
Mariner may be said to "act"; these are—the shooting of the Albatross;
the blessing of the water-snakes; and the biting of his arm. Each of
these actions has a very different character. The shooting of the Albatross comes quite suddenly and unexplained; superficially it is unmotivated and wanton. The Mariner himself never makes any explicit
attempt to explain it: nor does the poem contain, from his point of
view, any defence of it. We shall return to this. In the first phase of his
recovery, in the crisis at the centre of the poem, when he blesses the
water-snakes, he does so *unaware,* and this word "unaware" is deliberately repeated and occurs each time significantly, emphatically, at the
end of the line. That is to say, he did not really know what he was
doing; he could find no adequate spring of action in himself, and retro-
spectively attributed his undeliberate blessing to a supernatural influence on him:

> Sure my kind saint took pity on me.[24]

He himself thought he was more acted upon than acting. Against this
must be set the one clear occasion in the poem on which the Mariner
does deliberately act. In Part III, when all the crew, including himself,
have been stricken dumb by the drought, it is he who sees the sail; it
is he who, by a prodigious effort, bites his arm, sucks the blood and
finds voice to cry out. This is his one tremendous effort: it is a moment
of terrible hope for him and for the whole crew. But the hope is
blasted, not just negatively, but positively, appallingly, blasted. The
crew all die cursing him with their eyes, and he alone survives.

This is crucial to the whole poem's dramatic effect and, by inference,
also to its moral effect. On the one occasion when the Mariner does
consciously, deliberately and with all his effort *act,* his action leads
ironically to the climax of the disaster. The irony is enforced by the
two lines that end this Part:

> And every soul, it passed me by,
> Like the whizz of my cross-bow! [25]

The disastrous anticlimax of this action and this hope is made to
throw back to the earlier, unexplained act of the shooting. One main
element in the poem's theme is that the Mariner's experience involves

[23] Wordsworth's famous, disingenuous and ungenerous note on the "Mariner" was
published in *Lyrical Ballads* (1800), I, on an unnumbered page after the text;
quoted in full, Lowes, p. 520.
[24] l. 286.
[25] ll. 222-3.

a tangle of error, incomprehensibility and frustration. He is certainly not a great courageous spiritual adventurer, though he has a great spiritual experience. He started his voyage in unison with the ordinary world in a common set of values: he comes back as half outcast and half participator. In the poem as a whole a deliberate contrast is certainly presented between the background of the wedding and the Mariner's tale. The interruptions of the Wedding-Guest are meant to point this contrast. His constant fear is that the Mariner is a ghost come back from the dead or even himself some kind of infernal spirit. The contrast is not so much between two types of personality, the normal/conventional and the abnormal/adventurer, but between two aspects of reality, and two potentialities of experience, the visible bodily world of human beings marrying and giving in marriage and an invisible world of spirits and the dead where quite a different system of values is to be learnt. The effect of the interruptions of the Wedding-Guest is to show how these two kinds of reality are always co-existent: the total effect of the poem is to show them interpenetrating. As it has been said, in one aspect the poem is a prothalamium, and there is even the hint that though the wedding-guests who make the "loud uproar" have got their values wrong, yet the bride and bride-maids singing in the garden-bower are somehow touched by the Mariner's spiritual knowledge: and certainly the guest who has heard the tale cannot join the ordinary merry-making: "He went like one that hath been stunned."

The words "error" and "incomprehensibility," used just now of the Mariner's experience, were then a temporary and partial formulation of what must now be developed. The Mariner leaves his killing of the Albatross without any full explanation; he does not, cannot or dare not attempt to give his motives. But the description of the bird, its nature and power, taken with the prose gloss, makes it clear that the killing of it was a ghastly violation of a great sanctity, at least as bad as a murder. The bird's human associations appear in the fact that it was hailed as a Christian soul in God's name, it answered the Mariner's hollo, ate human food, and played with the crew. The gloss calls it "the pious bird of good omen." [26] Thus it images not only its own obvious place in the natural order, but a system of both human and religious values which is declared to have power over the ship and its crew through its connection with the weather. Furthermore, a function of the bird as a Christian emblem is also hinted at later on, when its corpse is hung round the Mariner's neck "instead of the cross."

[26] Coleridge's "Argument" to the edition of 1800 said the Mariner killed the bird "cruelly and in contempt of the laws of hospitality."

We have to consider our terminology for talking of an image used in such a complex way. Mr. Warren systematically and boldly uses the terms "symbol" and "symbolism," and develops his theory of a symbol as "focal, massive, and concrete"; Dr. Bowra also accepts the term "symbol." The terminology is not what matters so much as the degree of precision and equation that the use of a terminology allows. Mr. Warren is here somewhat confused: at one point he seems to equate the killing of the bird with the murder of a human being (arguing by a long analogy from Poe), and at another point to say that the killing "symbolises" the Fall. If these two things are to be held together, it is clear that the symbol must be functioning not merely towards different objects but in different ways: for the killing cannot *equate* with both a murder and the Fall, which are very different kinds of things. It seems best to avoid the term "symbol" in order to avoid this risk of incompatible equation. What happens in the poem is that the images gather their bearing by progressively rich associations, by gradual increment, and that exact equation is never fully demanded, even though the associations are ordered and controlled. The killing of the Albatross thus becomes a violation of a great sanctity at the animal, human, and spiritual levels: but these levels are only gradually declared as the poem proceeds, just as the Mariner only gradually discovered the consequences of what he had done. Our enlightenment runs parallel with his.

Any possible link with the Fall is of a different kind from the link with murder; for if such a link is there, it lies in the corruption of the human will by original sin and must be imported into the poem from outside, to explain the Mariner's motive, when he is not able or willing to explain it himself. His sin may or may not be partly the sin of pride and self-assertion against the order of the universe. As the poem stands it is a sin of ignorance, and links to that half-adumbrated sin of Cain, that he "neglected to make a proper use of his senses etc." It was a wicked ignorance because accompanied by a wildly thoughtless failure to consider what might be the truth about the order of the universe.

This failure to reach the truth, and, to him, the incomprehensibility of what was going on, is made more apparent when the rest of the crew become accomplices in his crime. They do not know whether the fog and mist (along with the Albatross who brought them) are good or bad, or whether the bird belongs more to them or to the breeze: nor do they know whether the sun is good or bad. This is made fully apparent in that wonderful pair of stanzas in which the thought and verse are in shape identical, but with opposite content:

And I had done a hellish thing,
And it would work 'em woe:
For all averred, I had killed the bird
That made the breeze to blow.
Ah wretch! said they, the bird to slay,
That made the breeze to blow!

Nor dim nor red, like God's own head,
The glorious Sun uprist:
Then all averred, I had killed the bird
That brought the fog and mist.
'Twas right, said they, such birds to slay,
That bring the fog and mist.[27]

The best approach to clarifying these stanzas (and the poem as a whole) is through the nature of the sun.

In the very next stanza the misunderstanding and incomprehensibility are allied to the wonder at novelty which the poem took over from the sixteenth-century voyages:

We were the first that ever burst
Into that silent sea.

This is one of the places in which the parallel between the physical voyage and the spiritual experience is most perfectly realised. An experience you don't understand produces first a shock of new glorious delight and then turns out to be something else. It is the worst kind of ethical and spiritual mistake—accepting wrong values.

On the naturalistic level this turns on the character of the tropic sun: and much here depends on the syntax.

Nor dim nor red, like God's own head,
The glorious sun uprist:

The syntax of these two lines makes it possible to interpret—

Either (a) That God's head *is* dim and red, but the glorious sun uprose
unlike it.
Or (b) That the glorious sun rose like God's head which is *not* dim
and red.

Interpretation (b) is made rather more likely, and (a) rather more unlikely, by the comma after "red," and this comma is apparently present in all texts. *Lyrical Ballads,* 1800, reads:

[27] ll. 91–102.

Nor dim nor red, like an Angel's head,

with a comma after "head." [28] There seems no apparent reason, either internally in the poem, or externally, why an angel's head should be dim and red. This temporary variant seems to point to accepting interpretation (b) with the common reading.

The very fact that Coleridge ever changed "God's own" to "an Angel's" seems to suggest that what he had in mind was the nimbus, aureole or "glory" of Christian iconography, and that this is picked up in the word "glorious." The rising sun was bright, golden and rayed, quite different from the small, clear-edged, bloody sun which becomes the image of evil two stanzas later. At the naturalistic level, both for the mariners and for Coleridge, the tropic sun changed from being a beautiful, pleasant, "good" thing to being an unpleasant, evil thing: this change is a natural quality of the tropic sun, irrespective of the eye of the beholder. The naturalistic error of the crew was not to know that the tropic sun has this double character: and this naturalistic error is an image of their moral and spiritual error. This brings clearly to the front a main feature of "the great appearances of nature" in the poem. It has been remarked for some time that the evil and disaster in the poem occur under the light of the sun, and the different phases of the redemption occur under the light of the moon. And Mr. Warren has developed this "symbolism of the two lights" further than it had been taken before, by the introduction of his "secondary" theme which I shall come to in a moment.

In Part II the becalming and the drought all occur under the influence of the sun; it is under the bloody sun that the deep rots, and that the creatures of the deep are slimy things that crawl with legs upon the slimy sea. We have already noticed how the spectre-bark appears in conjunction with the tropical sunset.

Part IV begins with the crisis of extreme isolation, with the frustrated desire for death, and then moves into the first phase of recovery and redemption.

The parallels here again between the spiritual and the natural—the physical imagery not just illuminating but actually conveying the

---

[28] *Lyrical Ballads* (1800), I, 162. The important comma after "Angel's head" is omitted in *PW*, I, 190, *apparatus criticus*. Warren at this point seems to be mistaken: he accepts interpretation (b) for the text, but then goes on to argue that the mariners have a wrong view of God because "dim and red" are qualities of the "other light" group, and belong with the luminous haze, etc. But surely "dim and red" are an anticipation of the evil "bloody sun" that soon follows. Warren is far too exact in requiring every "dim" light to be "good"; and he underestimates the truth to physical fact about the tropic sun. See also Leo Kirschbaum, *The Explicator*, Vol. VII, No. 1, Oct. 1948. I thank Mr. James Maxwell for this reference, which, in fact, introduced me to Warren's book.

spiritual state—are what most characterise the poem. It is clearest in
the landless waste of the sea, the most awful loneliness:

> Alone, alone, all, all alone,
> Alone on a wide wide sea!
> And never a saint took pity on
> My soul in agony.[29]

The transition also from the barren desire for death to the first state
of redemption is brought in through the magnificent imagery of the
moon and stars. From the helpless repetition of

> the sky and the sea, and the sea and the sky[30]

—the dead, static, unchanging monotony of the spiritual isolation
without a specified light—there is a shift by means of the wonderful
stanza

> The moving Moon went up the sky,
> And no where did abide:
> Softly she was going up,
> And a star or two beside—[31]

From death to life, or rather from death-in-life, which is so much
worse than death that death is longed-for and unattainable. From
death-in-life to life. From the flat, unchanging waste of the sea and the
sky and the sky and the sea to the ordered, even movement, with grace
and hope, of the moon and stars.

The prose gloss at this point is that one long sentence of astounding
beauty:

> In his loneliness and fixedness he yearneth towards the journeying
> Moon, and the stars that still sojourn, yet still move onward; and every
> where the blue sky belongs to them, and is their appointed rest, and
> their native country and their own natural homes, which they enter
> unannounced, as lords that are certainly expected and yet there is a silent
> joy at their arrival.

The emphasis there seems unmistakable; that the moon and the stars
express order and joy. And the word "joy" was a key word for Coleridge to express the fullest and richest happiness in experience.

By this moonlight we see the colouring of the water-snakes, and the
blessing of them is by this moonlight:

[29] ll. 232–5.
[30] l. 250.
[31] ll. 263–6.

> Beyond the shadow of the ship,
> I watched the water-snakes:
> They moved in tracks of shining white,
> And when they reared, the elfish light
> Fell off in hoary flakes.[32]

The beams of the moon have just before been said to fall "Like April hoar-frost spread." In Dorothy Wordsworth's Journal and again and again in Coleridge's descriptive prose this comparison between moonlight and hoar-frost or "hoariness" occurs. It was one of their common, agreed comparisons.

The blessing under moonlight is the critical turning-point of the poem. Just as the Albatross was not a mere bird, so these are not mere water-snakes—they stand for all "happy living things." The first phase of redemption, the recovery of love and the recovery of the power of prayer, depends on the Mariner's recognition of his kinship again with other natural creatures: it is an assertion and recognition of the other central principle in the letter to Sotheby:

> that everything has a life of its own, and that we are all *One Life.*

And at that point the reminder of the sin against this principle is gone—

> The Albatross fell off, and sank
> Like lead into the sea.[33]

At this point we must pause and look back; for we have passed over a difficulty in the imagery of the sun and moon. If the moon is to be associated always with the good and the redemption, why is it that the crew die by the star-dogged moon at the end of Part III? It is difficult to explain this and yet support the idea of a consistently developing imagery in terms of the penance and redemption and reconciliation theme alone; and it is this point, together with others allied to it, that chiefly made me sympathetic to the idea behind Mr. Warren's secondary theme of the "Imagination."

The poem up to this point, that is Parts I to IV and the opening stanzas of Part V, taken together with the ending, Part VII, is relatively easy to interpret as a tale of crime, punishment and reconciliation, with the recovery of love in the blessing of the water-snakes as its climax. But the remainder of Part V and the whole of Part VI do not seem at first sight to have quite the same coherence and point. It is here that readers may still find "unmeaning marvels" and an elab-

[32] ll. 272–6.
[33] ll. 290–1.

orated supernatural machinery which dissipates concentration. There are wonderful details in the verse, some of the finest descriptions of all; but they may seem to fall apart and to have too little bearing on each other and on the whole. Many published accounts of the poem do not adequately face the implications of the detail in these Parts. It is therefore best to summarise shortly what happens.

The Mariner hears a roaring wind and sees the fires and lightning in the sky. But the ship moves on untouched by the wind, and the re-animated dead men work it: a troop of blessed spirits has entered into them. These spirits make various music. The ship goes on, moved from beneath by the spirit of the South Pole. Through the Two Voices the Mariner learns that it is this Polar Spirit who requires vengeance for the Albatross's death, and that he will have more penance to do.

Part VI. The Voices say that the ocean is under the power of the moon. The ship is now moved northward by the angelic power while the Mariner is in his trance. He wakes to see the final curse in the eyes of the dead men. Then that spell is snapped, and he feels at last a sweet breeze on himself alone. He arrives at his home port, steeped in moonlight. Then, as the gloss says: "The angelic spirits leave the dead bodies, And appear in their own forms of light." This acts as the signal which brings out the boat from land.

In Part VII a dreadful rumbling sound comes under the water and the ship sinks.

A quite normally accepted and simple interpretation of Parts V and VI treats them as a further necessary extension of the expiation theme. In the blessing of the water-snakes the Mariner has reconciled himself to the creatures, but it remains for him to reconcile himself also with the Creator:[34] therefore he has to suffer once more (this time from the curse of the dead men's eyes) and to win the power of recognising the beauty of the angelic music.

This is broadly acceptable; but it takes us very little distance in understanding the complicated machinery. Is there any serious import in the answers to such questions as these: What is the function of the Polar Spirit? In one aspect he appears as the friend and avenger of the "pious bird of good omen," and yet he is made to work under obedi-ence to the angelic troop, who are thus plainly, in the spiritual hier-archy, superior to him; and he is bought off by the promise that the Mariner's penance shall continue. It might have seemed better to have made the angelic troop themselves the protectors of the Albatross and made them require the further penance. Why should the ship be moved first by the Polar Spirit and then by the angelic power? Again, what is the significance of the two winds in Parts V and VI? Put the

[34] See, e.g., Bowra, *op. cit.*, pp. 70–71.

problem in another way: are the avenging by the tutelary spirits of the South Sea and the reanimation of the dead bodies to work the ship here just out of politeness, because Wordsworth suggested them?[35] The first main problem here is to decide whether there is any meaning in the two different kinds of supernatural being.

The whole discussion of this problem has been clarified and ennobled by Mr. Warren's long essay, which I now wish to summarise. He maintains that the poem has "two basic themes, both of them very rich and provocative." The primary theme, which is "the outcome of the fable taken at its face value as a story of crime and punishment and reconciliation," is "the theme of sacramental vision, or the theme of the 'One Life.'" The secondary theme is "concerned with the context of values in which the fable is presented" and is "the theme of the imagination." The two themes are finally fused in the poem.[36] He aims to establish the existence of this secondary theme by two lines of argument—first, that there are parts of the poem not otherwise easily intelligible, such as Parts V and VI; and second, that the symbolism of the poem is richer and more coherent than the redemption, visionary, theme alone requires. Mr. Warren elaborates the contrast of the "two lights" in great detail.

He points out quite rightly and fully (p. 87) [p. 30 in this volume] the "pervasive presence of the moon and moonlight in Coleridge's work," especially in association with creativeness. In "Sonnet to the Autumnal Moon," 1788, she is called the "Mother of wildly-working visions," [37] and in "Songs of the Pixies," 1796, "Mother of wildly-working dreams." [38] "Christabel" and "The Ancient Mariner" are bathed in moonlight: the moon is over the deep romantic chasm of "Kubla Khan"; it is prominent in "The Nightingale," "Cain" and "Dejection."

Mr. Warren maintains that the association is so recurrent and persistent in Coleridge's writing, between creation or the activity of the secondary imagination and the moonlight, half-lights, dim lights, gloom, luminiscent clouds and so on, that the association between them can justifiably be regarded as habitual; and that as it goes back even into his very early poems, it can without injustice be taken as estab-

---

[35] The Fenwick Note to "We are Seven," *Poetical Works,* ed. E. de Selincourt, I, 360–61; see also Lowes, pp. 222–23.

[36] Warren, p. 71. [See this volume, pp. 21–22.]

[37] l. 2; *PW,* I, 5.

[38] Warren here gives the publication date; the lines were written in 1793; *PW,* I, 40–4. The phrase quoted is in fact applied to Night, not to the Moon; ll. 85–7 are more relevant:

> What time the pale moon sheds a softer day
> Mellowing the woods beneath its pensive beam:
> For mid the quivering light 'tis ours to play.

lished (even if not consciously) at the time of writing the "Mariner." He quotes from the *Biographia* passage in which Coleridge recalled the origin of the *Lyrical Ballads* themselves:

> The sudden charm, which accidents of light and shade, which moon-light or sun-set, diffused over a known and familiar landscape, . . . These are the poetry of nature.[39]

The Albatross, besides being associated with human nature on the level of the primary theme, is also associated with the moon, mist, cloud and fog-smoke, on the level of the secondary theme of the imagination:

> In mist or cloud, on mast or shroud,
> It perched for vespers nine;
> Whiles all the night, through fog-smoke white,
> Glimmered the white Moon-shine.[40]

Furthermore the bird is associated with the breeze, which Mr. Warren takes to be the "creative" wind, for which there are countless parallels in other poets.

> The sun is kept entirely out of the matter. The lighting is always indirect, for even in the day we have only "mist or cloud"—the luminous haze, the symbolic equivalent of moonlight. Not only is the moon associated with the bird, but the wind also. Upon the bird's advent a "good south wind sprung up behind." And so we have the creative wind, the friendly bird, the moonlight of imagination, all together in one symbolic cluster.[41]

He thus establishes what he calls a "symbolic cluster," including the wind, bird, mist and moon, which belong to the imagination and all the imaginative side of man's activity. And in his shooting, the Mariner not only commits a crime against the other, natural and spiritual, order of the world, but also a crime against creative imagination; and part of the penalty is the loss of the wind.

The dual character of the ice which I have already noted at the first arrival of the ship near the South Pole—the emerald and the dismal sheen—also expresses the dual character of the imagination, that it is partly a blessing and partly a curse to him who lives by it. It is this cursing side of the imagination which accounts for the particular vengeance of the Polar Spirit on the Mariner as distinct from the punishment exacted by the sun. And this dual character and special vengeance also explain why the moon is allowed to be the light by which

[39] *BL*, II, 5.
[40] ll. 75–8.
[41] Warren, p. 91.

the crew die. And further, in his capacity of Wanderer, the Mariner is to be thought of as the "cursed poet" of the later Romantics. By contrast to the moon and mist of the Imagination, the sun and the glaring light are, for Mr. Warren, the light of the Understanding, the mere reflective faculty, which "partakes of DEATH";[42] and just as the Mariner and also the crew failed to see the significance of the bird in the mist, so they also fail to understand the nature of the sun, not only at the naturalistic level, as we have already seen, but also because they are taking the lower faculty of the Understanding as their inadequate guide to life.[43]

Warren's essay must be read complete, with its notes, to see how inadequate is this broad outline of its argument. There are two main questions about it which most urgently need asking: how far does it succeed in giving a coherent and convincing explanation of the miscellaneous detail in the difficult parts of the poem? And in what sense does it establish that there is a theme which *is* "the theme of the imagination"? The answers to both these questions depend upon the view we take of symbols and symbolism.

I suggest that if we accept the term "symbol" we must allow symbols a freer, wider, less exact reference; and that therefore it is probably wiser to drop the term altogether. Mr. Warren himself fully allows for the possibility (even likelihood) that Coleridge did not *consciously* use symbols at all. This is consistent with Coleridge's recognition of the unconscious element in the workings of genius: but it does not therefore follow that there was a latent precision waiting for critics to elucidate it. Mr. Warren seems in the last resort to be a precisionist more because he wishes to make clear to himself and others some features of the richness he has found in the poem than because he believes that the poem actually works upon its readers by the methods of precision. There is a natural and proper dread of the long-traditional praise of the poem's "atmosphere," because that praise has so often accompanied the belief that there is scarcely any content or meaning at all, and that all is thin, vague and "magical." But a rich certainty is not the only alternative to a poor uncertainty.

The first of the two questions, that about the miscellaneous detail, can only be answered here by two examples. In dealing with Part V,

[42] Warren, p. 79 and *passim,* quoting *BL,* I, 98. [See this volume, p. 30.]

[43] Assuming that the sun does represent the Understanding, I think Mr. Warren makes his own case more difficult than he need when he comes to explain the appearance of the sun in a good context, when the angelic spirits fly up from the bodies into it. For surely to Coleridge the Understanding was never altogether unnecessary in the whole scheme of the mind's action. It was never altogether superseded, but was always a necessary ground of advance towards the Reason and the Imagination.

Warren agrees with Bowra and others that "in the reanimation of the bodies of the fellow mariners, there is implicit the idea of regeneration and resurrection"; but then he finds himself compelled to write:

> But the behaviour of the reinspirited bodies, taken in itself, offers a difficulty. Taken at the natural level, the manipulating of the sails and ropes serves no purpose. Taken at the symbolic level, this activity is activity without content, a "lag" in the poem, a "meaningless marvel." [44]

Nor does he later succeed in giving an adequate explanation of the need for this behaviour, even when not "taken in itself"; for he concentrates more on the angelic troop than on what it makes the bodies do.

At this point Warren's scheme of symbolism does not serve us. But if we look to the total effect of the poem on its readers, there is little doubt that ll. 329–44 add something not adequately expressed elsewhere, especially the stanza:

> The body of my brother's son
> Stood by me, knee to knee:
> The body and I pulled at one rope,
> But he said nought to me.

This brings home, as nothing else does, the horror of the deaths, the violation of family ties which the action has involved; it dramatises to the Mariner's consciousness the utter ruin of the merry, unified community which had set out on the voyage. The curse in the stony eyes (ll. 436–41) is made far more appalling by this specially intimate experience of the fact that intimacy was gone for ever. And this is achieved at a point where the "system" of the poem is decidedly weak.

The second point of detail is the rumbling and the sinking of the ship in Part VII; Warren skates over this rather hastily:

> There is the terrific sound which sinks the ship and flings the stunned Mariner into the Pilot's boat. In the logic of the symbolic structure this would be, I presume, a repetition of the wind or storm motif: the creative storm has a part in re-establishing the Mariner's relation to other men. Even if the destruction of the ship is regarded, as some readers regard it, as a final act of the Polar Spirit, to show, as it were, what he could do if he had a mind to, the symbolic import is not altered, for the Spirit belongs to the cluster of imagination which has the terrifying and cataclysmic as well as benign aspect.[45]

He then argues that the sinking of the ship is not an act of the Polar Spirit, but of the angelic troop.

[44] Warren, p. 97. [See this volume, p. 38.]
[45] Warren, p. 100. [See this volume, p. 41.]

At the level of the primary theme, the angelic troop wipe out the crime (i.e., the "criminal" ship and the dead bodies); at the level of the secondary theme, they do so by means of the "storm" which belongs to the symbolic cluster of the imagination.[46]

But this is surely to abandon a coherent symbolism altogether and to fall back on simple interpretation of the narrative in the light of decisions already made; for the clusters of symbols established earlier have borne some intelligible relation (either traditionally or in Coleridge's habitual associations) to what they symbolise: the creative wind is traditionally intelligible, and the moon and half-lights have special associations for Coleridge. But the method of the ship's destruction does not conform to the "logic" of such symbolism as this; and Warren's use of "I presume" points to his uneasiness about it.[47] A submarine rumbling followed by a violent explosion is in a different key; it has a different sort of effect on the reader from that of the other items which Warren groups together as associated with the Imagination.

What seems to have happened is that Mr. Warren, delighted by the relative coherence of the moon-bird-mist-wind cluster, has forced other items into congruence with it, by minimising differences in their character and in their emotional effects. But such forcing would not have been necessary if he had started out with a less rigid theory of symbolic reference. That his own mind was working from the less precise towards the more precise, even in the course of thinking out his essay, is apparent in the way he speaks of the light of the sun. On p. 93 [p. 34 in this volume] he writes of the sun:

It is the light which shows the familiar as familiar, it is the light of practical convenience, it is the light in which pride preens itself, it is, to adopt Coleridge's later terminology, the light of the "understanding," it is the light of that "mere reflective faculty" that "partook of Death."

His mind is here moving out of what is richly and variously suggestive into what is precise and technical. I suggest that he went through a similar mental process in reaching the interpretation of the moon, the bird and the mist, and that in the result the "theme of the imagination" is something narrower and more technical than the poem can carry. For by the imagination Warren does mean the technical, creative poet's imagination of Coleridge's later theory, and he says (p. 103) [p. 44 in this volume] that the poem is "in particular about poetry itself." This leads to the conception of the Mariner as the *poète maudit*.

[46] *ibid.*
[47] And his writing of the Mariner being flung into the boat by the sound suggests some hasty reading here.

The fact, however, is that there was for Coleridge no such stable and exact association between moonlight, half-light, shifting lights-and-shadows, etc. and the specifically poetic and creative imagination. These were indeed associated with and productive of creative and visionary moods, but they were also associated with the more tender emotions and the more fruitful virtues, such as those of love. These lines, addressed to Tranquillity in 1801

> And when the gust of Autumn crowds,
> And breaks the busy moonlight clouds,
> Thou best the thought canst raise, the heart attune,
> Light as the busy clouds, calm as the gliding moon.[48]

are part of the definition of a mood of moral insight which originally had a topically political context. This description of Hartley in a letter to Tom Poole in 1803 is expressive of the creativeness of a child's whole living personality, which may indeed bear analogies to poetic creativeness but yet, in a child, certainly cannot be identified with it:

> Hartley is . . . a strange strange Boy—*"exquisitely wild"*! An utter Visionary! Like the Moon among thin Clouds, he moves in a circle of Light of his own making—he alone, in a Light of his own. Of all human Beings I never yet saw one so naked of *Self*.[49]

Again, the famous lines of "Dejection: an Ode"

> This light, this glory, this fair luminous mist,
> This beautiful and beauty-making power[50]

describe not the "shaping spirit of Imagination" itself, but the Joy which is the prerequisite condition of it. One more example brings us back closely to Mr. Warren's more limited application of the "symbolism" of the moon. In the lines "To William Wordsworth," written after hearing the first version of *The Prelude* read aloud, Coleridge describes himself while listening as being like the sea under the influence of the moon:

> In silence listening, like a devout child,
> My soul lay passive, by thy various strain
> Driven as in surges now beneath the stars,
> With momentary stars of my own birth,

---

[48] *PW*, I, 361.
[49] *UL*, I, 292.
[50] *PW*, I, 365.

> Fair constellated foam, still darting off
> Into the darkness; now a tranquil sea,
> Outspread and bright, yet swelling to the moon.[51]

Here there is no doubt that the moon is an image of Wordsworth's imagination seen in its power over others. By contrast, at the other extreme of reference, is the Note-Book entry

> Socinianism, moonlight; methodism, a stove. O for some sun to unite heat and light! [52]

And in the intermediate, neutral area Coleridge once summed up his fascinated interest in the natural phenomena of a night-sky by applying to it the phrase of Boccaccio, *vestito d'una pallidezza affumicata*.[53]

It would be endless to quote all Coleridge's uses of imagery from the moon and stars, clouds, the night-sky and uncertain lights; these examples give some idea of the range. It is certain that, before and after the time of "The Ancient Mariner," such images were used for creativeness both of a wider and of a more specially poetic kind; but they were used also for much else, especially in conjunction with the subtler processes of the mind and the more delicate modes of feeling. They were used especially for the mysteries and uncertainties of mental life which Coleridge was beginning to explore more fully as he became more dissatisfied with the crude associationism represented by Hartley and its "inanimate cold world," and as his general ideals of life moved further from those of "the poor loveless ever-anxious crowd." It seems to me that the imagery of the mist and the moon and the Albatross in "The Ancient Mariner" belongs with this area of experience in general and with Coleridge's exploration of it; indeed the whole poem is part of the exploration, it is part of the experience which led Coleridge into his later theoretic statements (as of the theory of the Imagination) rather than a symbolic adumbration of the theoretic statements themselves.

Within the poem, and most obviously in the motto later added from Burnet ("Harum rerum notitiam semper ambivit ingenium humanum, nunquam attigit." [54]), the emphasis is on the mystery and the richness

---

[51] ll. 95–101; *PW*, I, 408. Cf. Satyrane's First Letter in *The Friend*, 23 Nov. 1809, quoted in *PW ad loc*. The patches of phosphorescent light in the sea-foam are an image of Coleridge's troubled, but bright, reception of those moments in *The Prelude* in which he himself was involved.

[52] *AP*, p. 26.

[53] *ibid*., p. 46.

[54] "Ever about the knowledge of these things circles the thought of man, never reaching it."

of the mystery. Through the development of the imagery we are gradually led into the realisation that the values of "the land of mist and snow" are of the greatest possible concern, but that they are indescribable. They are certainly contrasted with the values which belong to the specious day-to-day clarity of the sun, but they are left to establish themselves in us mysteriously and indefinitely, as Burnet's world of spirits is mysterious and indefinite. Mr. Warren has permanently enriched our understanding of the poem by insisting on its statement of the "context of values" in which the crime and punishment and reconciliation occur; his symbolist "equations" serve to point out elements which may be involved in this context; but the decision to "adopt Coleridge's later terminology" in stating the equivalents symbolised has, in the long run, the effect of making the poem seem more technical and diagrammatic than Mr. Warren himself first found it, or than Coleridge could ever have admitted it to be.

The Mariner and the Albatross

by George Whalley

> For me, I was never so affected with any human Tale. After
> first reading it, I was totally possessed with it for many days—
> I dislike all the miraculous part of it, but the feelings of the
> man under the operation of such scenery dragged me along
> like Tom Piper's magic whistle.[1]

In these words, in a letter to Wordsworth dated January 30, 1801,
Charles Lamb spoke of Coleridge's *The Rime of the Ancient Mariner*.
Some readers continue to echo Mrs. Barbauld's complaints that the
poem is improbable and has an inadequate or distasteful moral. But
these are mental reservations: poetry of the order of *The Ancient
Mariner* does not work its magic upon the mind alone; and mental
afterthoughts are of little use in explaining, least of all in explaining
away, the profound spiritual and emotional effect of this poem. For
every sympathetic reader since Lamb has been similarly possessed and
haunted by *The Ancient Mariner*.

Lamb's criticism is remarkable in a contemporary. The incisiveness
of his comment, however, lies not so much in his sensitivity to the
fascination of the poem as in his immediate recognition of human
feeling as being central in it. Lamb understood and loved Coleridge,
and was never to free himself of the fascination of the man: " 'the
rogue has given me potions to make me love him' "[2]; " 'tis enough to
be within the whiff and wind of his genius, for us not to possess our
souls in quiet."[3] Unfortunately we have not the means of knowing

---

"The Mariner and the Albatross" by George Whalley. From University of Toronto Quarterly, *XVI (1946–1947) pp. 381–98. Abridged version from Kathleen
Coburn, ed.,* Coleridge: A Collection of Critical Essays (*Englewood Cliffs: Prentice-
Hall, Inc., 1967), pp. 32–50. Reprinted by permission of the author, the University
of Toronto Press, and Prentice-Hall, Inc. Quotations and references revised by
permission of the author.*

[1] *Letters of Charles and Mary Lamb,* ed. E. V. Lucas (London, 1935), I, p. 240.

[2] *Ibid.,* I, p. 185.

[3] *Ibid.,* II, p. 191.

that "provocative and baffling personality" as Lamb did. But a close and sympathetic reading of the *Rime* will bring us much nearer to the essential Coleridge than one would expect in a poem that is professedly "a work of pure imagination."

The Rime of the Ancient Mariner is less "a fantasticall imagination and a drowsie dreame" than "a continued allegory, and a darke conceit." There is an important letter of Coleridge's which confirms the allegorical interpretation of the poem: "I have often thought, within the last five or six years, that if ever I should feel once again the genial warmth and stir of the poetic impulse, and refer to my own experiences, I should venture on *a yet stranger and wilder Allegory than of yore*—. . . ." It is difficult to see how the missing factor in the comparative could be anything but *The Ancient Mariner;* and the opinion is confirmed by the associated idea that follows: "that I would *allegorize* myself, as a Rock with it's summit just raised above the surface of some Bay or Strait in the Arctic Sea, . . ." [4] Although the early action of the poem and the killing of the albatross take place in the Antarctic Sea, the details derive from the literature of Arctic travel, as Lowes has shown and as Coleridge would certainly remember.

I wish to examine the poem (a) to show how and to what extent Coleridge's inner life is revealed in the *Rime;* and (b) to show that the albatross was for Coleridge, whether consciously or unconsciously, a symbol with profound personal significance.

I

The aesthetic and poetic qualities of *The Ancient Mariner* are impressive. . . .

Without in any way detracting from the value of *The Rime* as a poem, I wish to show that the "haunting quality" grows from our intimate experience in the poem of the most intense personal suffering, perplexity, loneliness, longing, horror, fear. This experience brings us, with Coleridge, to the fringes of madness and death, and carries us to that nightmare land that Coleridge inhabited, the realm of Life-in-Death. There is no other single poem in which we come so close to the fullness of his innermost suffering. The year after the composition of *The Ancient Mariner* he gave the self-revealing image of

> some night-wandering man whose heart was pierced
> With the remembrance of a grievous wrong,

[4] *Collected Letters of Samuel Taylor Coleridge,* ed. E. L. Griggs (Oxford, 1956, 1959), IV, p. 975; II, p. 262; dated [November, 1819?].

> Or slow distemper, or neglected love,
> (And so, poor wretch! filled all things with himself,
> And made all gentle sounds tell back the tale
> Of his own sorrow).[5]

Many years later he told how "from my very childhood I have been accustomed to *abstract* and as it were unrealize whatever of more than common interest my eyes dwelt on; and then by a sort of tranfusion and transmission of my consciousness to identify myself with the Object—. . ." [6] Whether or not he recognized this process at the time, Coleridge enshrined in *The Ancient Mariner* the quintessence of himself, of his suffering and dread, his sense of sin, his remorse, his powerlessness. And

> Never sadder tale was heard
> By man of woman born.[7]

For it is not only a crystallization of his personal experience up to the time of the composition of the first version, but also an appalling prophecy fulfilled to a great extent in his life and successively endorsed by his own hand as time passed.

II

Life-in-Death is a recurrent theme in Coleridge's thought. In *The Ancient Mariner* it is luridly personified:

> Her lips were red, her looks were free,
> Her locks were yellow as gold:
> Her skin was as white as leprosy,
> The Night-mare Life-in-Death was she,
> Who thicks man's blood with cold.

And when he summarizes his life in 1833 in his own epitaph, he beseeches the passer-by to

> lift one thought in prayer for S.T.C.
> That He, who many a year with toilsome breath
> Found Death in Life, may here find Life in Death.

---

[5] "The Nightingale: A Conversation Poem. April, 1798."

[6] *Collected Letters*, IV, pp. 974–75. This passage immediately precedes the passage quoted above (note 4).

[7] 1798 version. Unless otherwise indicated, quotations from the poem follow the 1834 version.

Life-in-Death meant to Coleridge a mixture of remorse and loneliness.
Yet "loneliness" is perhaps too gentle and human a word; let us say
"aloneness." It is precisely this combination of remorse and aloneness
with which the Mariner's experience is steeped. Remorse is an emotion
easy to find in the poem. It is also broadcast throughout Coleridge's
letters and later poems, and requires no detailed consideration here.
The Mariner's aloneness is directly stated:

> Alone, alone, all, all alone,
> Alone on a wide wide sea!
> And never a saint took pity on
> My soul in agony.

It is thrown into relief by contrast with multiplicity:

> The many men, so beautiful!
> And they all dead did lie:
> And a thousand thousand slimy things
> Lived on; and so did I.

And it culminates in the horror of utter solitude:

> O Wedding-Guest! this soul hath been
> Alone on a wide wide sea:
> So lonely 'twas, that God himself
> Scarce seeméd there to be.

The same theme recurs in smaller details. When the spirits leave the
shipmates' bodies, it is with the sound of birds and "like a *lonely* flute."
The "Spirit from the south pole" is a *lonesome* spirit; and, even
though there is an air of self-sufficiency in the phrase "who bideth by
himself," like so many solitary people—like Coleridge, like Dorothy
Wordsworth—he loves birds:[8]

> He loved the bird that loved the man
> Who shot him with his bow.

When the spectre-bark has sailed away and the Mariner has snapped
the spell of the dead seamen's eyes, he looks out over the ocean and
feels a sense of foreboding

> Like one, that on a *lonesome* road
> Doth walk in fear and dread.

These details have a cumulative effect in heightening the direct statement of the Mariner's desolation.

[8] For Coleridge on birds, see note 27 below.

The Mariner's isolation is not "the wages of sin" so much as the state of sin.

> I looked to heaven, and tried to pray;
> But or ever a prayer had gusht,
> A wicked whisper came, and made
> My heart as dry as dust.

Or again:

> The pang, the curse, with which they died,
> Had never passed away:
> I could not draw my eyes from theirs,
> Nor turn them up to pray.

As will be shown, the same aloneness haunted Coleridge and echoes like doom through his other poems, his letters, the Notebooks. And in the passionate eloquence of his morbid remorse, he is constantly and restlessly seeking the sin at the root of the desolation: finding as alternative sins his indolence, "abstruse research," the failure of his marriage, the opium habit.

The "Moon gloss" forges a powerful link between the Mariner and Coleridge.

> In his *loneliness and fixedness* he yearneth towards the journeying *Moon*, and the stars that still sojourn, yet still move onward; and every where the *blue sky* belongs to them, and is their appointed rest, and their *native country* and their own *natural homes,* which they enter unannounced, as lords that are certainly expected and yet there is a *silent joy at their arrival.*[9]

The gloss was written some time between 1800 and 1817, and may have been under revision until the completion of the 1829 collection. It is Coleridge's personal and mature comment upon *The Ancient Mariner.* The "Moon gloss" itself contains the essence of his loneliness and homelessness, feelings which were acutely present long before the composition of *The Ancient Mariner.*

In "Frost at Midnight" (1798) Coleridge recalls the sense of isolation he felt as an orphan at Christ's Hospital:

> if the door half opened, and I snatched
> A hasty glance, and still my heart leaped up,
> For still I hoped to see the *stranger's* face,
> Townsman, or aunt, or sister more beloved. . . .

[9] My italics.

> For I was reared
> In the great city, pent 'mid cloisters dim,
> And saw nought lovely but the sky and stars.

In January, 1796, we find him writing to the Reverend T. Edwards:

> I have got among all the first families in Nottingham, and am marvel-
> lously caressed—: but to tell you the truth I am quite home-sick—aweary
> of this long long absence from Bristol—I was at the *Ball,* last night—and
> saw the most numerous collection of handsome men & Women, that I
> ever did in one place; but alas! the faces of Strangers are but moving
> Portraits—... I feel as if I were in the long damp Gallery of some
> Nobleman's House, amused with the beauty or variety of the Paintings,
> but shivering with cold, and melancholy from loneliness.

Six months before the composition of the *Rime,* we find him telling
his brother that

> at times
> My soul is sad, that I have roamed through life
> Still most a stranger, most with naked heart
> At mine own home and birth-place.

And in January, 1798, he wrote: "The first sunny morning that I walk
out, at Shrewsbury, will make my heart die away within me—for I
shall be in a *land of Strangers!*" With the last important recrudescence
of his creative genius, he was to write in 1802 a curious echo of the
watersnake passage:

> All this long eve, so balmy and serene,
> Have I been gazing on the western sky,
>   And its peculiar tint of yellow green:
> And still I gaze—and with how blank an eye!
> And those thin clouds above, in flakes and bars,
> That give away their motion to the *stars;*
> Those stars, that glide behind them or between,
> Now sparkling, now bedimmed, but always seen:
> Yon crescent *Moon,* as fixed as if it grew
> In its own cloudless, starless lake of *blue,*
> *I see them all so excellently fair,*
> *I see, not feel, how beautiful they are!* [10]

It is important to notice in the "Moon gloss" the association of the
Moon, the blue sky, and home. Elsewhere the same combination of
symbols, sometimes with the addition of tree(s), is associated with the
thought of home, friendship and love, or their absence.

---

[10] "Dejection: An Ode"; composed April 4, 1802. My italics.

Practically speaking Coleridge was homeless for the greater part of his life. Remembering the number of times he must have exhausted the patience of his hosts to the point of serious misunderstanding and even the breach of friendship, the last part of the "Moon gloss" is given pathetic personal significance by comparison with "Youth and Age" (1823–32).

> Where no hope is, life's a warning
> That only serves to make us grieve,
> When we are old:
>
> That only serves to make us grieve
> With oft and tedious taking-leave,
> *Like some poor nigh-related guest,*
> *That may not rudely be dismist;*
> *Yet hath outstayed his welcome while,*
> *And tells the jest without the smile.*

In thinking of nature as a healer, he notes (1811) the fate of the desolate man: again his thought turns to home, and the parallel with the "Moon gloss" is again striking.

> And even when all men have seemed to desert us and the friend of our heart has passed on, with one glance from his "cold disliking eye"—yet even then the *blue heaven* spreads it out and bends over us, and the little tree still shelters us under its plumage as a second cope, a *domestic firmament,* and the low creeping gale will sigh in the heath-plant and soothe us by sound of sympathy till the lulled grief lose itself in *fixed gaze* on the purple heath-blossom, till the present beauty becomes a vision of memory.[11]

And in October, 1803, he is trying to account for his aloneness. "But yet, . . . , the greater & perhaps nobler certainly all the subtler parts of one's nature, must be solitary—Man exists herein to himself & to God alone/—yea! in how much only to God—how much lies *below* his own Consciousness!" [12]

Let us see how this sense of homelessness is imaged in the Mariner. When the ship finally reaches port he cries:

> Oh! dream of joy! is this indeed
> The light-house top I see?
> Is this the hill? is this the kirk?
> Is this mine own countree?

---

[11] *Anima Poetae,* ed. E. H. Coleridge (London, 1895), pp. 246–47. My italics.

[12] *The Notebooks of Samuel Taylor Coleridge,* ed. Kathleen Coburn (London, 1957, 1959), Vol. I, entry 1554, October, 1803.

This utterance is charged with the deep thankfulness of the seafarer returned. In many a page of his travel books Coleridge had read of the emotions aroused by sighting the home port after a long voyage; and he is able to reproduce the feeling, mingled joy and pathos and fear, because he has experienced it imaginatively. In December, 1796, he had anticipated in a striking manner the Mariner's return: "The Sailor, who has borne cheerily a circumnavigation, may be allowed to feel a little like a coward, when within sight of his expected & wished for port." [13] Although the Mariner is returning to his "own countree," one feels sure that he does not expect anybody to be waiting for him.

> The Pilot and the Pilot's boy,
> I heard them coming fast:
> Dear Lord in Heaven! it was a joy
> The dead men could not blast.

Returned from the dead, Lazarus-fashion, he is overjoyed to see living people, to hear their voices. But there is a characteristic note of homelessness when he says

> O sweeter than the marriage-feast,
> 'Tis sweeter far to me,
> To walk together to the kirk
> With a goodly company!—
>
> To walk together to the kirk,
> And all together pray,
> While each to his great Father bends,
> Old men, and babes, and loving friends
> And youths and maidens gay!

It is an impersonal picture, pregnant with the sense of isolation. There are "loving friends" but they do not seem to be his; the "old men" are not his brothers or his father, the "youths and maidens gay" are not his children. We catch an overtone of words spoken by him on a grimmer occasion:

> O happy living things! no tongue
> Their beauty might declare:

words uttered with the same sense of isolation in which Coleridge wrote some twenty-five years later

> And I the while, the sole unbusy thing,
> Nor honey make, nor pair, nor build, nor sing.[14]

[13] *Collected Letters,* Vol. I, p. 263.
[14] "Work without Hope"; composed February 21, 1825.

Not only are the Mariner's spiritual and emotional experiences similar to, if not identical with, those we know Coleridge to have suffered, but there is rather more than a hint that the drawing of the Mariner is a self-portrait. The Mariner's two salient characteristics are his glittering mesmeric eye, and his passivity. The Mariner says,

> I move like night from land to land,
> I have strange power of speech.

The first line is not only a reflection of Coleridge's isolation, but also a vivid metaphoric description of his imaginative wanderings while reading "like a cormorant" before composing *The Ancient Mariner*. We have Lamb's evidence for Coleridge's "strange power of speech" even at school. "How have I seen the casual passer through the Cloisters stand still, entranced with admiration (while he weighed the disproportion between the *speech* and the *garb* of the young Mirandula), to hear thee unfold, in thy deep and sweet intonations, the mysteries of Jamblichus, or Plotinus . . . , or reciting Homer in his Greek, or Pindar—. . . ." Even the hostile Hazlitt could write, in 1818: "That spell is broke; that time is gone for ever; that voice is heard no more: but still the recollection comes rushing by with thoughts of long-past years, and rings in my ears with never-dying sound."

The Mariner's passivity is Coleridge's too; and the significance of that word (as of "pathos," "patience," "sympathy") is rooted, in more than the etymological sense, in suffering. In those deeply moving observations of the night sky noted in early November, 1803,[15] all written at about two o'clock in the morning, the elements of passivity, suffering, and the moon meet; while finally, in a similar entry made in Malta eight months later, all combine with the longing for home and for Asra: "The glorious evening star coasted the moon, and at length absolutely crested its upper Tip/ . . . It was the most singular & at the same time beautiful Sight, I ever beheld/O that it could have appeared the same in England/at Grasmere." In these entries we see a man who is waiting, capable still of feeling; and he is driving down the intolerable suffering only by the *fixedness* with which he gazes on the sky.[16] Sometimes there must have shaped in his mind the blasphemy that he expunged from the *Rime* after 1798: that "Christ would take

---

[15] *The Notebooks*, ed. Coburn, Vol. I, entries 1622, 1624, 1625, 1627, 1628, 1635, 1648, 1649, 1650; cf. 1674, 1681; Vol. II, entry 2139 quoted in text.

[16] Cf. an amusing parallel in *Collected Letters*, I, 658: "In truth, my Glass being opposite to the Window, I seldom shave without cutting myself. Some Mountain or Peak is rising out of the Mist, or some slanting Column of misty Sunlight is sailing cross me/so that I offer up soap & blood daily, as an Eye-servant of the Goddess Nature."

no pity on My soul in agony." [17] And the Mariner's prayer must often
have been repeated in those long nights:

> O let me be awake, my God!
> Or let me sleep alway.

At the height of the Mariner's suffering and loneliness, sleep and
dream become central ideas. It is noticeable that the Mariner, like
Coleridge, does not regard them as necessary concomitants. The Mariner, it is true, hears the "two voices in the air" while he is asleep; but
he recognizes them as being merely voices so that the tempo of the
verse does not race as it did when he sighted the spectre-bark. His
prayer on entering harbor shows that the whole voyage has been, in a
real and horrible sense, a dream; when he hears the Pilot approaching
his pulse quickens because the dream of the voyage is broken by a
breath of solid human reality. Coleridge conceived sleep to be, in its
essence, dreamless. We have his own evidence for the fact that his life
(like the Mariner's voyage) passed in a state of dream;[18] and that there
were times, *after* the composition of *The Ancient Mariner,* when the
dream, the thing imagined, was more solid and terrible than "the normal realities of life." "While I am awake, by patience, employment,
effort of mind, & walking I can keep the fiend at Arm's length; but the
Night is my Hell, Sleep my tormenting Angel. Three Nights out of
four I fall asleep, struggling to lie awake—& my frequent Night-
screams have almost made me a nuisance in my own House. *Dreams
with me are no Shadows, but the very Substances & foot-thick Calami-
ties of my Life.*" [19] It is the dreams which accompany his sleep that are
the torment and horror. Remove the dreams from his sleep and he
would not "fall asleep, struggling to lie awake." And the Mariner's
craving and prayer for sleep are paralleled by Coleridge before 1802,
and are more insistently repeated after that date.

The first version of *The Ancient Mariner* was completed for publication in *Lyrical Ballads* in 1798. . . . The final version of *The Ancient
Mariner* is the outcome of at least twenty years of reflection, no matter
how sporadic the reflection may have been. That can only mean that

---

[17] *Ibid.,* II, 1202: "55 days of literal Horror [at sea], almost daily expecting and
wishing to die"; and *Ibid.,* IV, p. 673: "I longed for Death with an intensity that
I have never seen exprest but in the Book of Job—"
[18] See the dream-epitaph, *Ibid.,* II, 992:

> Here sleeps at length poor Col, & without Screaming
> Who died, as he had always liv'd, a dreaming:
> Shot dead, while sleeping, by the Gout within,
> Alone, and all unknown, at E'nbro' in an Inn.

[19] *Ibid.,* II, p. 991.

the poem continued to hold for him the personal significance with which it was charged at its creation.

In the course of revision the symbolism has been sharpened, not least of all by the gloss; the personal context has been clarified; and, most important of all, the whole poem has been confirmed in the light of his later life.

III

It is misleading to think of Coleridge's life as falling into three distinct phases: one of turbulent preparation, one of cloudless creation, and one of disappointment and broken imagination. The brief creative period, 1797–9, emerges from a mind more hopeful than in the later period; but it is essentially the same mind—restless, mercurial, morbid, remorseful, fearful. For a short time he was lifted up (though on no constant wings) by his marriage, by the birth of Hartley, by his intimacy with William and Dorothy Wordsworth. But even such "fecundating" happiness, a happiness ominously stressed in the letters of the period, was not able to change the thing that was Coleridge. The early period foreshadows the later. In 1796 he had written: "There is one Ghost, that I *am* afraid of; with that I should be perpetually haunted in this cursed Acton, the hideous Ghost of departed Hope." [20] In the same year he observed that

> Such a green mountain 'twere most sweet to climb,
> E'en while the bosom ached with loneliness—. . . .[21]

In the spring of 1797 he told Cottle: "On the Saturday, the Sunday, and the ten days after my arrival at Stowey I felt a depression too dreadful to be described. . . . Wordsworth's conversation, &c, roused me somewhat; but even now I am not the man I have been—and I think never shall. A sort of calm hopelessness diffuses itself over my heart." Early in 1797 he had anticipated *The Ancient Mariner* by telling his brother George that "I have roamed through life/Still most a stranger," and that "To me the Eternal Wisdom hath dispensed/A different fortune and more different mind." As early as 1795 he had referred to the taking of drugs;[22] and in the spring of 1798 *Kubla*

---

[20] *Collected Letters,* I, 272.

[21] "To a Young Friend."

[22] The earliest letter, of 1791 (*Collected Letters,* I, p. 18), is inconclusive, but is linked by E. H. Coleridge with a letter of March, 1795 (*Ibid,* I, p. 188), where almost nightly doses of opium are mentioned. But see also Lowes, *The Road to Xanadu,* rev. ed. (Boston, New York, 1930), pp. 415, 415n., 604i.

Khan was conceived "in a profound sleep, at least of the external senses." All the elements of the later broken Coleridge are noticeably present by 1797. Coleridge was too intelligent and introspective a man to fail to notice them and understand, at least dimly, their import.

Before the date of the composition of *The Ancient Mariner* the sense of personal doom was present to Coleridge, even though at times, and for lengthy periods, he was able to "keep the fiend at Arm's length." It has been shown that the acute consciousness of his aloneness and home-lessness was already present, foreshadowing the "Moon gloss" and the pitiful threnody "Youth and Age." The *Rime* is the projection of his own suffering, of his sense of personal danger, his passivity, his perplex-ity. At first he projected himself unconsciously into the poem by the intensity with which he imaginatively experienced the Mariner's situa-tion. During the voyage from Gibraltar to Malta he had an opportunity not only to verify his "observations" of the sea, but also to know what it was to pass "55 days of literal horror almost daily expecting and wishing to die." The time in Malta was a critical, desolate period; and I believe that in Malta Coleridge realized more vividly than ever before that he trembled on the brink of inactivity, of dream, of fatal procras-tination, of creative impotence. It is this realization that he projects into the 1817 version of *The Ancient Mariner*: the personal allegory is sharpened by the gloss, and the addition of important details relates the Mariner's experience more intimately with Coleridge's experience of opium.[23]

Fundamentally it is the personal quality of the poem that accounts for its vivid haunting fascination. And that effect is much heightened when we recognize the prophetic power of the poem; when we know that Coleridge himself in later life recognized the poem for a personal allegory and endorsed its prophecy by a life of wandering loneliness and suffering.

IV

The central figure of the albatross remains to be considered; for "the albatross . . . binds inseparably together the three structural princi-ples of the poem: the voyage, and the supernatural machinery, and the unfolding cycle of the deed's results." [24] Nothing less than an intensely personal symbolism would be acceptable against the background of such intense suffering. The albatross must be much more than a stage

[23] See Bald, "Coleridge and *The Ancient Mariner*," pp. 33ff.
[24] Lowes, *The Road to Xanadu*, p. 221.

property chosen at random or a mechanical device introduced as a motive of action in the plot.[25] The albatross is the symbol of Coleridge's creative imagination, his eagle.[26]

It was Wordsworth, not Coleridge, who thought of the albatross. Whether Wordsworth or Coleridge actually stumbled upon the albatross, in Shelvocke or anywhere else, does not matter. In November 1797, the final element, around which the whole poem would crystallize, was needed. As Lowes has shown, Coleridge, in all his diverse and obscure reading before *The Ancient Mariner*, read with the falcon's eye "which habitually pierced to the secret spring of poetry beneath the crust of fact": it is as though he knew intuitively what he needed without knowing exactly what he was looking for. It would be valuable to have a verbatim record of the dialogue during that momentous walk through the Quantock Hills, rather than the retrospective and somewhat patronizing report made by Wordsworth nearly fifty years after the event.

Coleridge would notice at once that the albatross was mechanically suitable: it would fit naturally into a voyage to Antarctic regions; sailors are superstitious about birds and indeed have special superstitions about the albatross; and he may even have noticed that it was amenable to rhyming in a way that other alternatives may not have been. But apart from practical considerations of plot or versification, the albatross was exactly what Coleridge was looking for. It was a rare species of bird,[27] of exceptional size,[28] solitary, haunting a limited and strange and, for Coleridge, evocative zone, harmless yet by tradition

[25] Cf. *ibid.*, p. 303. Lowes emphasizes the *triviality* of the deed and suggests that Coleridge required a trivial deed to set the punishment in motion. Clarke ["Certain Symbols in *The Rime of the Ancient Mariner*," in *Queen's Quarterly*, XI (1933), 29] dismisses the possibility of the albatross as symbol.

[26] Cf. T. S. Eliot, *The Use of Poetry and the Use of Criticism* (London, 1933), p. 69, where the eagle is used as the symbol of the creative imagination. Coleridge also seems to be using the symbol in an epigram of 1807 in reply to Poole's encouragement: "Let Eagle bid the Tortoise sunward rise—As vainly Strength speaks to a broken mind" (*Complete Poetical Works*, ed. E. H. Coleridge, II, p. 1001). Cf. Shelley's description of Coleridge as "a hooded eagle among blinking owls."

[27] Coleridge's keen interest in birds is shown by his foot-note to "This Lime-Tree Bower," and by a MS. note in a copy of Gilbert White's *Works* (quoted in *Coleridge: Select Poetry and Prose*, ed. Stephen Potter, p. 719): "I have myself made by collection [?] a better table of characters of Flight and Motion" (of birds). See also *Anima Poetæ*, pp. 178, 193, 194.

[28] The giant albatross probably would occur to Coleridge's mind. Notice Wordsworth's mention of "wingspan of 12 or 13 feet." But see Lowes, *The Road to Xanadu*, pp. 226–27 and 529, for the "feasible" species; and Bald, "Coleridge and *The Ancient Mariner*," 6: "Saw a . . . Boy running up to the Main Top with a large Leg of Mutton swung, Albatross-fashion, about his neck." (*Notebooks*, II, entry 1997.)

beneficent. Some or all of these facts would, I suggest, flash through Coleridge's mind; and he at once seized upon the albatross as the right (or, at the very lowest valuation, an adequate) symbol for his purpose.

Coleridge was a confirmed symbolist. In 1815 he wrote: "An *idea,* in the highest sense of that word, can not be conveyed but by a *symbol.*" [29] Ten years before, he had noted how

> In looking at objects of Nature while I am thinking, as at yonder moon dim-glimmering thro' the dewy window-pane, I seem rather to be seeking, as it were *asking,* a symbolical language for something within me that already and forever exists, than observing any thing new. Even when that latter is the case, yet still I have always an obscure feeling as if that new phænomenon were the dim Awaking of a forgotten or hidden Truth of my inner Nature/ It is still interesting as a Word, a Symbol! It is Λόγος the Creator! and the Evolver! [30]

The process he describes here is not a newly acquired practice, but an innate and habitual attitude of mind. *The Ancient Mariner* is what it is for the reason that Coleridge has clearly given: because in that poem he found what he was "seeking, as it were *asking* for," long before the date of the Notebook entry—"a symbolical language for something within me that already and for ever exists." Furthermore Coleridge was not the man to use words or symbols without consideration or to select them carelessly. In an entry, touched with more humility than this single sentence would suggest, he said in 1805: "few men, I will be bold to say, put more meaning into their words than I or choose them more deliberately & discriminatingly." [31]

That the link between the albatross and the creative imagination grows out of the inner necessity of the poem and of the man can be verified by only one passage in the *Rime.* The evidence is extremely nebulous, but, being possibly primary evidence, should not be overlooked. The shipmates' first judgment on the killing of the albatross was that the Mariner had

killed the *bird*
That made the *breeze* to blow.

Late in 1806 Coleridge connects Genius and the wind: "Tho' Genius, like the fire on the Altar, can only be kindled from Heaven, yet it will

---

[29] *Biographia Literaria,* Chap. IX.

[30] *Notebooks,* II, entry 2546; dated April 14, 1805. See also *Anima Poetae, op. cit.,* p. 225; ". . . words are not mere symbols of things and thoughts, but themselves things, and . . . any harmony in the things symbolized will perforce be presented to us more easily, as well as with additional beauty, by a correspondent harmony of the symbols with each other."

[31] *Notebooks,* II, entry 2372.

perish unless supplied with appropriate fuel to feed it—or if it meet not with the virtues, whose society alone can reconcile it to earth, it will return whence it came, or at least lie hid as beneath embers, till some *sudden & awakening Gust of regenerating Grace* αναξωπυρει, re-kindles and reveals it anew." [32] And the symbol of the imagination, or of inspiration, is frequently, outside Coleridge's writing,[33] a bird.

Far more important is Coleridge's reply to the celebrated strictures of Mrs. Barbauld. *The Ancient Mariner,* he said, "ought to have had no more moral than the Arabian Nights' tale of the merchant's sitting down to eat dates by the side of a well, and throwing the shells aside, and lo! a geni starts up, and says he *must* kill the aforesaid merchant, *because* one of the date-shells had, it seems, put out the eye of the geni's son." [34] The tone of the retort is jocular. If the *Rime* had for Coleridge the personal significance that I believe it had, it would be difficult for him to reply other than jocularly. About seven years before the reply to Mrs. Barbauld, he tells a correspondent exactly how he reacts to a situation of that kind.

My sentiments on the nature of all *intrusions into private Life,* and of more private *personalities* in all shapes I have given at large in the Friend, and yet more pointedly in the Literary Life. . . . These you know, but you cannot know my dear Sir! . . . how many causes accumulating thro' a long series of years, and acting perhaps on constitutional predisposition, have combined to *make me shrink from all occasions that threaten to force my thoughts back on* myself *personally—as soon as any thing of this sort is on the point of being talked of, I feel uneasy till I have turned the conversation,* or fairly slunk out of the room—. . . .[35]

Coleridge's facetiousness in speaking of the moral of *The Ancient Mariner* was misleading, as it was intended to be; but it both hides and contains the clue we are looking for.

The nature of the Mariner's crime is thrown into high relief by Coleridge's italics (*must, because*): and with it, the nature of Coleridge's personal "crime"—for so he regarded it in later life. The identity is then complete.

[32] *Notebooks,* II, entry 3136. My italics. This parallel is offered with caution.

[33] But see note 29 above for an example in Coleridge's writing. *Notebooks,* II, entry 3182 is also of interest: "The moulting Peacock with only two of his long tail-feathers remaining, & those sadly in tatters, yet proudly as ever spreading out his ruined fan in the Sun & Breeze." This may be a direct observation; but, from the context, it appears likely that Coleridge is noting a personal metaphor.

[34] *Table Talk,* May 31, 1830.

[35] *Unpublished Letters,* II, p. 274. Coleridge italicized the words "personalities" and "myself." Other italics are mine.

The crime was at the same time wanton and unintentional.[36] The Mariner shoots "the *harmless* albatross," and "*inhospitably* killeth the pious bird of good omen," having no conception of the implications of his deed. The Mariner *could* have withheld his arrow, the merchant his date-shell; but neither saw any reason for doing so. Certainly the Mariner learned a sharp lesson about killing birds before the voyage was done; but that lesson was of no service to him when, in a moment of idleness or boredom, he aimed his cross-bow at the albatross. "But so it is! Experience, like the stern lanthorn of a Ship, casts it's light only on the *Wake*—on the Track already past." [37] There is the sternness and inexorability of Greek tragedy in the paradox that an act committed in ignorance of the laws governing albatrosses and genii *must* be punished in the most severe manner.

That Coleridge regarded his own suffering in precisely this light is clear from a poem written as early as 1803.

> Such punishments, I said, were due
> To natures deepliest stained with sin,—
> For aye entempesting anew
> The unfathomable hell within,
> The horror of their deeds to view,
> To know and loathe, yet wish and do!
> *Such griefs with such men well agree,*
> *But wherefore, wherefore fall on me?*

"The Pains of Sleep" is saturated with the same confusion and perplexity that the Mariner experienced. The sin from which the suffering arose was committed in the same way: "Tho' before God I dare not lift up my eyelids, & only do not despair of his Mercy because to despair would be adding crime to crime; yet to my fellow-men I may say, that I was seduced into the ACCURSED Habit ignorantly." [38] Even though he may have suspected, when it was too late, what would be the outcome of his struggle with "this body that does me most grievous wrong," Coleridge did not know, when the process began, that he was killing his eagle. The act was wanton: yes, in the sense that it was unnecessary, that it could have been avoided. And it is that very

---

[36] Bald ("Coleridge and *The Ancient Mariner*," 39ff.), in interpreting this passage, is concerned to explain the *amoral* attitude as a characteristic of opium reverie. Lamb notes the same quality without attributing it to opium.

[37] *Unpublished Letters*, II, p. 354. E. H. Coleridge (in *Coleridge: Studies by Several Hands*, eds. E. Blunden and E. L. Griggs, p. 41) notes the first appearance of this "stock sentence" as January 2, 1800.

[38] *Collected Letters*, III, p. 476. Coleridge is here thinking specifically of the opium habit, which he probably recognized as a symptom and not the "sin" itself. He is here replying to Cottle who considered opium to be central.

knowledge—afterwards—that the act could, perhaps easily, have been avoided, if at the very beginning he had understood the implications of his action, that makes stark tragedy both in Coleridge's life and in the Mariner's voyage.

> O had I health and youth, and were what I once was—but I played the fool, and cut the throat of my own Happiness, of my genius, of my utility. . . .[39]

> Well would it have been for me perhaps had I never relapsed into the same mental disease; if I had continued to pluck the flowers and reap the harvest from the cultivated surface, instead of delving in the unwholesome quick silver mines of metaphysic lore. And if in after-time I have sought a refuge from bodily pain and mismanaged sensibility in abstruse researches, which exercised the strength and subtilty of the understanding without awakening the feelings of the heart; still there was a long and blessed interval, during which my natural faculties were allowed to expand, and my original tendencies to develop themselves;—my fancy, and the love of nature, and the sense of beauty in forms and sounds.[40]

The interval was a good deal shorter and less blessed than he was prepared to remember in 1815. And there was a great deal more in the two apparently naïve verses of moral than Mrs. Barbauld could have guessed, more even than Coleridge was willing to remember when, long after their writing, he was asked for an explanation.

When the process of the atrophy of his creative imagination, foreshadowed in *The Ancient Mariner*, was far advanced and Coleridge felt that his life was sinking "in tumult to a lifeless sea," he wrote his comment upon that process. The lines are some of the most desolate ever written.

> But now afflictions bow me down to earth:
> Nor care I that they rob me of my mirth;
>   But oh! each visitation
> Suspends what nature gave me at my birth,
>   My shaping spirit of Imagination.
> For not to think of what I needs must feel,
>   But to be still and patient, all I can;
> And haply by abstruse research to steal
>   From my own nature all the natural man—
>   This was my sole resource, my only plan:
> Till that which suits a part infects the whole,
> And now is almost grown the habit of my soul.[41]

---

[39] *Ibid.*, III, 73–74. February 17, 1808.

[40] *Biographia Literaria*, Chap. I.

[41] "Dejection: An Ode," lines 82–93; "Dejection" is itself echoed in "To William Wordsworth" (1807).

V

The Ancient Mariner, in addition to its other unique qualities, is both an unconscious projection of Coleridge's early sufferings and a vivid prophecy of the sufferings that were to follow. The poem was probably not originally intended to be a personal allegory: but that is what, in Coleridge's eyes, it became later as the prophecy was slowly, inexorably, and lingeringly fulfilled.

As far as I know *The Ancient Mariner* has never been interpreted as a personal allegory. To do so (and the evidence for it is weighty) not only gives a clue to the source of the poem's intensity but also explains beyond cavil its moral implications. *The Ancient Mariner* is, however, of primary importance *as a poem;* and no specialized interest—moral, biographical, or allegorical—can be allowed to assail the integrity to which, as a poem, it is entitled. But the interpretation I have suggested does bring the reader into intimate contact with Coleridge the man. Even to attempt to understand him will induce sympathy, and from sympathy some understanding can grow.

Carlyle's judgment of Coleridge is harsh and grossly unsympathetic: "To steal into heaven . . . is forever forbidden. High treason is the name of that attempt; and it continues to be punished as such." [42] Yet Coleridge had written:

> I dare affirm, that few men have ever felt or regretted their own infirmities, more deeply than myself—they have in truth preyed *too* deeply on my mind, & the hauntings of Regret have injured me more than the things to be regretted.[43]

> For years the anguish of my spirit has been indescribable, the sense of my danger *staring,* but the conscience of my GUILT worse, far far worse than all!—I have prayed with drops of agony on my Brow, trembling not only before the Justice of my Maker, but even before the Mercy of my Redeemer. "I gave thee so many Talents. What hast thou done with them?" [44]

> And as to what *people* in *general* think about me, my mind and spirit are too awfully occupied with the concerns of another Tribunal, before which I stand momently, to be much affected by it one way or other.[45]

---

[42] Thomas Carlyle, *The Life of John Sterling;* in *Complete Works of Thomas Carlyle* (New York, 1853), XX, p. 60.
[43] *Collected Letters,* III, p. 337.
[44] *Ibid.,* III, p. 476.
[45] *Unpublished Letters,* II, p. 424; November 9, 1828.

Carlyle's judgment overlooks the quantity and quality of the work Coleridge did complete; overlooks the fact that Coleridge throughout his life was dogged by physical disease; overlooks the fact that Coleridge became a man tormented and haunted, at times beyond the capacities of desire or effort, by the knowledge that the eagle had visited him, that he had inhospitably killed "the pious bird of good omen," and that it might well have been otherwise.

The Sad Wisdom of the Mariner

by A. M. Buchan

Among the "great defects" that Wordsworth discovered in "The Ancient Mariner" when it was grudgingly reprinted in the second edition of the *Lyrical Ballads,* was the fact that the Mariner "does not act, but is continually acted upon." [1] He gave the poem credit for stanzas in which beautiful images appeared, but as he preferred passion to imagery and avoided the kind of "outrageous incident" to be found in Coleridge's work, he excluded "Christabel" from the publication and retained "The Ancient Mariner" only with an apology. The critics have been kind in calling his attitude "ungracious," especially as Coleridge had been not only a partner in the enterprise but the more active editor of both editions. They have been mistaken, however, in trying to argue that Wordsworth was as wrong-headed in his judgment as he was selfish, because there seems to be little doubt that the inaction of the Mariner, as well as the presence of much imagery and strange incident, is a significant mark of the poem.

The Mariner, in fact, is the least active creature in the series of incidents through which he is carried. He exerts himself on several occasions, in laying his hand on the Wedding Guest and detaining him by his story from the marriage ceremony, in shooting the Albatross, in hailing the spectre-ship, in blessing the water-snakes,—though for this act he gives credit to his kind saints,—and, near the end of the voyage, in working on a rope with the dead crew and taking the oars of the pilot's boat so as to help row it to land. Through most of what befalls him, however, he is the passive victim of forces more active than he, and the observer of events that determine his fate without his participation.

"The Sad Wisdom of the Mariner" by A. M. Buchan. From Studies in Philology, *LXI, No. 4 (October, 1964), 669–88. Copyright © 1964 by the University of North Carolina Press. Reprinted by permission of the publisher.*

[1] *Letters of Samuel Taylor Coleridge,* ed. E. L. Griggs, I, 602.

A storm drives the ship in which he sails towards the south, and masses of polar ice enclose it. The Albatross, whose coming opens the ice-pack, eats and plays of its own free choice, and a helmsman steers the ship into the open. After the Mariner shoots the bird, his comrades accuse him and then free him of blame and then again condemn him by hanging the bird's dead body around his neck. Across the becalmed sea comes a spectre-ship gliding without breeze or tide of its own inner motion, and the utmost the Mariner can do is hail it with a cry and then realize how horribly deceitful has been the joy aroused in his companions. On the spectre-ship Death and Life-in-Death dice for his soul, and he stands idly watching. In the ship's shadow the water-snakes move and are beautiful, and he blesses them, though without knowing why; and, as he does so, the Albatross, which he has made no effort to untie, drops from his neck.

A wind blows, the ship moves, the dead men rise and man the ropes, and, for an instant of action, he joins them in their work. But, beyond his power to interfere, the ship is urged on by a wind and a spirit, and other spirits discuss him and decide his fate while he lies asleep. As they near the land, the ghosts of the dead men signal to the shore, while the Mariner only watches them. By no purpose or struggle of his own he finds himself in the sea and then in the pilot's boat being rowed to land, and the movement of his lips and his grasp at the oars terrify those who have come to save him. As he wanders from place to place, it is not of his own will that he tells his story, even to the Wedding Guest, but because he is driven by an anguish he can neither understand nor restrain.

The sun and moon, the storm and wind, the Albatross and water-snakes, the men on the ship and the men in the pilot's boat, spirits and human beings and creatures of the sea and air are all actively compounding his fearful destiny, and, except for one or two actions not one of which is willed or justified or approved, he watches, suffers, endures, accepts. He has no reason for shooting the Albatross and no desire to do harm, and yet he is blamed for it. He wants to announce the happy news of the other ship's coming and does so at the price of his blood, but what a ship it is that comes! Even the impulse to bless the water-snakes is not his but the boon of kind saints who take pity on him. When he joins the dead sailors in working the tackle, the other man on the rope, his nephew, will not speak to him. In the pilot's boat, when he ventures to open his mouth, they think he is the Devil and draw back from him in terror. Though he pleads with the hermit to shrive him, the holy man is loath to agree, and the

Mariner, whose every act has turned to evil or been regarded as sinister, continues to bear the blame for what he has not chosen or approved of.

Through these strange events in which he is being "acted upon," as Wordsworth said, his senses are preternaturally alive to the shape, color, and sound of every object that presses in on him. When he leaves the harbour and returns to it, he remarks on the rocky hill, the lighthouse and the church with the weathercock on the steeple. He records the color of ice and fog and sky, the deadly colors of the lips and hair of Life-in-Death, the "rich attire" of the water-snakes and the crimson shadows of the ghosts of the dead sailors. Noises of every kind beat in on his mind, from the growling of ice and the whisper of the spectre-ship to the gentle voice of a spirit and the angelic chorus of the signallers. Though he does not act, he is always in the centre of motion, being driven like the ship before the gale or like a dreamer pursued by a fiend. Near him are men who drop like lead to the boards of the deck and snakes that move and rear and coil and swim. The blowing wind lifts his hair, and the dry sails sigh in its path. He is pitched to the deck by the sudden movement of the ship, and, after the rain comes, appears to float lightly in the air. Like a dead body he is cradled by the sea when the ship goes down. Twice he sleeps and once he dreams, and all the while, like the eyes of the pilot's boy, he moves to and fro. Like a dreamer he sees figures that seem outside and unrelated and yet in which he is intimately and disastrously involved. While everything occurs beyond his own will, it is his action that is being judged and his will that is held accountable.

Only in feeling is he a true participator in the world of light, color, sound and movement through which the incidents of the voyage carry him. With the other members of the crew he is merry as the ship leaves harbor, and fearful when the ice-pack grips them. Like them he welcomes the arrival of the Albatross, and then, for some dreadful unknown reason, he kills it. He revels in their rapid motion before the fair breeze and then dreads the utter silence of the calm. He is filled with excitement when another ship appears, a speck on the horizon, and his excitement changes to horror and disbelief when its ghastly open planks and more ghastly crew become clear. Terror closes in through the thick night, and, as his companions drop dead, an agony of solitude and disgust overwhelms him. In the lovely upward movement of the moon and the flash of the water-snakes he gains a quick, ecstatic joy and, in the sleep that comes, a feeling of peace and blessing. Fear returns when the crewmen arise to handle the rigging, till again it is released in an outburst of happiness over the song of the spirits gathered around the mast. When the ship rides into harbor, he sobs with joy, and even the weird spectacle of the spirits erect on the corpses of the crew cannot dim his happiness. Yet he shares the hermit's apprehension at the unnatural and fiendish look of the vessel, and the gladness of coming home is swamped in an agony of longing to pour out his terrible story. Even while he talks to the Wedding Guest, the comforting sound of the vesper-bell and the deep contentment of going to church with friends are shrouded in the memory of the godless terror of the sea. Like the motion of the ship in the clutch of the spirit, he goes "backwards and forwards" from mood to mood on a scale from the highest pitch of joy to a deep and utter despair.

All the things his senses know are clear, sharp, brilliant, and more so when they are terrifying. What his emotions are, as they swing in a wide arc this way and that, he also vividly understands. But why he acts, and why his actions are unforeseeable and doomed, is a mystery, though they seem in a hidden way to be bound up inextricably with every vivid bit of his experience.

To equate this inactivity, vivid sensory life and tumultuous emotion with similar tendencies in Coleridge is an obvious temptation. The parallel is on the surface, and the many and varied symbols may be interpreted in a number of ways. As the central figure of a great poem, however, the Mariner has first of all a life of his own, and speaks to mood and emotion and dimly-felt thought that are not necessarily those easily traceable in the man who imagined the tale. The first duty of criticism, as Coleridge wrote, is to examine "what has ipso facto pleased, and to what faculties or passions or habits of the mind they may be supposed to have given pleasure" [2] and, while the word "pleasure" is a strange one to apply to this harrowing imaginative journey, the "habits of the mind" to which the record appeals are not very difficult to discover. And the most direct approach to them may be found in a glance at the few actions of the Mariner, because in them lies a clue to the strange and mysterious universe in which they take place.

The one with which the poem begins and ends, the anguished desire to tell his tale, might be taken as a rite of confession for the expiation of his sin. Unfortunately for such a view, no hint is given that the hermit is willing to shrive his fearsome penitent, and the confession, if made at all, falls short of achieving its purpose. For the Mariner, though he is convinced of his sin, is far from clear about what it may be. The other person, the Wedding Guest, is

---

[2] *Ibid.*, II, 830.

certainly as unfit a confessor as Chaucer's friar. He is rude and
impatient with the crazy man who detains him from the wedding
feast, and he becomes abjectly terrified as the tale proceeds, suspect-
ing his companion of being one of the unearthly creatures he talks
about. He is, indeed, a very common ordinary fellow, picked out
for some obscure reason to hear the old man's yarn, and yet, after
he has heard it, he turns away from the festivities of the wedding
that are still going on, and awakes next morning sadder and wiser.
And why is he "sad" on account of having heard the tale? Why
is it no longer possible for him to join the merry group around the
bride and bridegroom?

His first shock comes when the Mariner answers the startled
question, "Why look'st thou so?" in the bare remark "With my
crossbow/I shot the Albatross." Abruptly the Wedding Guest is
plunged into an utterly bewildering world, not the familiar one of
things done because one wants to, such as getting married and going
to church, but a world of action without reason or justification. To
the common man, as to the Wedding Guest, such an act is completely
terrifying if it is conceivable at all. An evil deed he can account for
by any of the deadly sins about which he has been taught, as when
he explains the death of Abel by a hate and jealousy he feels within
himself. If an act is good and still beyond the scope of reason, the
common man utters the word "miracle" and is content to let it be.
The miracle of goodness he has heard about, but miraculous evil is
beyond the power of man to credit except by the agency of devils,
and the death of the Albatross is a miracle of evil. If such an act
can occur, sanity is threatened and the moral law disappears. For its
existence in the hands of man opens up the ghastly prospect that at
any moment he may suddenly realize that, by this one thing he has
done, though he did not intend or wish it to be done, irretrievable
evil has come to pass. Here, sharp and bright and horrifying and complete, is such an act,—"I shot the Albatross." In the stark phrase
lurks, even for the ordinary imagination, the stereotyped image of
the murderer staring in bewilderment at the weapon in his hand,—
the rock, the knife, the gun, the crossbow,—not yet believing he has
used it and to such deadly purpose.

Almost as shocking is the Mariner's way of loosening his lips and
parched tongue in order to give the tidings of the sail on the horizon.
The other crewmen accept the limitations of their dry lips and stand
agape, but he bites his flesh and sucks the blood and so becomes a
fearsome creature, saint or devil, who for the sake of announcing a
message, does violence to the flesh. However the act is interpreted, as
a clutch at a special insight or a mere devil's trick, the fact about it

is its enormity and, in the grim outcome of the burst of joy it arouses, its worse than uselessness. As the shooting is an act, unpremeditated and unmeant, that nevertheless must be accounted for, the cry "A sail! A sail!" is one born in pain and an inhuman effort of will that results in an ecstasy of hope doomed to be immediately shattered. It has been sealed in blood, and the imagery of blood accentuates its consequences. It heralds the coming of the bloodless skeleton, Death, and his companion Life-in-Death, who "thicks man's blood with cold." It is followed by the gloom of the thick night and the dim stars that drains the blood from the heart as from a cup. The biting of the arm is an act that, like all the ceremonial blood-letting which man has been guilty of in announcing a "something in the sky," serves merely, after a brief flurry of excitement, to close the ring of fear around him.[3]

When the Mariner next abandons his inaction to bless the water-snakes, the act, done "unaware," takes its meaning from the mood of despair preceding it. After the disappearance of the spectre-ship, the Mariner lives through a week of horror, disgust, and loneliness. His two hundred crew-mates drop dead, and the corpses lie sweating on the deck as if life still flowed through them. But they are not alive, as the Mariner knows only too well from the curse in their staring eyes. Only he and loathsome creatures in the ocean live on in the solitude. He pities himself, wishing he too were dead. As he watches the moon rise, he becomes aware of a brilliant panorama of light around him, the white gleam of the moon on the sea, the charmed red of the water in the ship's shadow, the spectral colors of the snakes.

> Blue, glossy green, and velvet black
> They coiled and swam; and every track
> Was a flash of golden fire,

and, in a flash as bright and golden within himself, he finds the snakes no longer loathsome but "happy living things." From the death of self-pity he moves into a love for the beautiful creatures around him, and, in blessing them, loses the burden of the Albatross.

Though they give only a respite from the fate that pursues the Mariner through the ice, the tropic heat, and the stagnation of the

[3] The sacrificial nature of this symbolism is made clear in "The Wanderings of Cain," a prose fragment being composed by Coleridge around the time he wrote "The Ancient Mariner." It appears in *Poetical Works of Samuel Taylor Coleridge*, ed. E. H. Coleridge (1912), I, 285–292. The prose account goes thus: "he [Cain] meets in the desart [sic] a young man whom upon a nearer approach he perceives to be Abel. . . . He is going to offer sacrifices . . . and persuades Cain to follow him . . . Abel offers sacrifice from the blood of his arm . . . he then persuades Cain to offer sacrifice, for himself and his son Enoch by cutting his child's arm and letting the blood fall from it."

ocean, the joy and the act of blessing are among the happy mysteries
of common experience that even the Wedding Guest may understand.
They are unwilled and beyond reason, the happiest of man's instinctive responses to the world of the senses, and yet the moment of delight never fails to relieve the burden of human fear. Though death
and rottenness remain and purpose dries out in dismal failure and
prayer is hopeless, the flash of delight at the mere gorgeous vividness
of things may cancel for an instant the mood of self-pity. The Mariner
is utterly alone and a sharer in the "body of this death." He is on
the verge of learning that mysterious and omnipotent spirits govern
his destiny. He is still charged with a crime he did not want to commit and for which he feels responsible none the less. Even so, the
water-snakes are beautiful, the air radiant with life, and from the
stiff bodies on the deck a troop of spirits sing angelic music. Though
he will always go in fear and dread, after this moment of joy and
blessing a light and crimson colors signal to the land toward which
he is being driven.

He takes part in two more actions, and in both he seeks a way
out of solitude back among men who work and move. As the crew
trim the vessel to bring it to land, he finds himself hauling on a
rope alongside his nephew. That he has a relative in the crew is
a startling fact, though he mentions it by the way. He wonders
how the ship moves without a wind, is aghast at the lifeless motions
of the crew, stands knee-to-knee by the body of his nephew, "But he
said nought to me." Again the Wedding Guest cries out in fear, because his strange companion has consorted with the dead and even the
dead have refused him a word. He and they share a futile and meaningless routine, since their effort is not needed to make the vessel
move, but, unlike the sailors who sing and talk together at such a
task, they are utterly silent. Theirs is a Sisyphaean labor like that of
the dwellers in hell. The Mariner, alone on a ship that needs no
human hand to guide and control it, joins a dead crew in deathly
motions, estranged from the one person on board who might know
and speak to him. In this fearful universe every act he performs is
without meaning.

He tries one last venture before the voyage ends. After he has
been picked up by the pilot, he moves his lips to talk and picks up
the oars to help the boat to land. The effect is ghastly,—the pilot
falls down in a fit, the hermit begins muttering a prayer of exorcism,
and the pilot's boy goes mad, sure that the passenger is the devil
himself. The hermit, who shakes with fear as he leaves the boat, has
doubts that the Mariner is a human being, and it is to answer his
doubt that the tale is told for the first time. With a holy man unsure,

what is the Wedding Guest to think of his persistent companion? "He went like one that hath been *stunned*/And is of sense forlorn," and the word "stunned" puts Mariner and Wedding Guest inseparably together. As the ship came into the harbor, a dreadful sound smote sky and ocean, split the bay, and sent the ship down like lead. It stunned the Mariner, leaving him afloat and senseless on the water. So the Wedding Guest is stunned, as he turns away from hearing the tale, and, in the single word, the experience of the Mariner becomes that of the common man who is made to share it.

As the tale ends, the Wedding Guest is persuaded of the reality of this universe in which sound and light and color, the massive sensory powers of the mind, are infinitely more important and effective than common day-by-day actions, such as going to church or a wedding. Over that vivid and primitive realm of the senses preside the equally massive emotions of man,—fear and ecstasy, the cheerful beginning of a journey and its frightening end in loneliness and death, man's abiding sense of guilt and his moments of occasional relief. Now and then the objects of sense by their very beauty enable man to be blessed and to lose his conviction of sin, but he is caught up again in the hands of great spirits of air and sea that mete out an ineluctable destiny. Into this chaotic world of sense and feeling man slips when he dreams and recognizes then its power over him, but it is also present when he is awake, though comforting patterns of common sense hide and explain away its inexplicable power. His every act is governed by it, the brutal deed of which he is ashamed and for which he pays the penalty of remorse as well as the gesture of instinctive sympathy and kindliness. While he lives with his senses drinking in color and movement and light and sound, he feels and acts by their insistent pressure rather than by reason and will. With the Mariner he journeys over a sea of sensation in which God does not seem to be, because the forces presiding over it are not the ordinary moral and practical laws of common sense. Its ruling genius is the brilliant and ghastly figure of Life-in-Death,

> Her lips were red, her looks were free,
> Her locks were yellow as gold:
> Her skin was as white as leprosy,

—a woman passionate, seductive, loathsome in her loveliness, and free as are all things in nature of the moral scruple that haunts mankind.

The sad wisdom that came to the Wedding Guest and may be felt by the sensitive reader of the Mariner's tale has little directly to do with any conventional moral theme of absolution or of kindness to living things or of the virtue of worshipping in church with a company of goodly folk. These are the familiar answers to the Mariner's dilemma and he gives them his approval, but he knows his plight to be too hopeless for any common sort of penance or relief. He has prayed and the burden of the Albatross has fallen from his neck, but he must continue to suffer the life-in-death that the spirits of air and water have doomed him to. In his loneliness he has learned how blessed it is to have friends near, and he has gained compassion for all things great and small, but he must be for ever leaving human company and seeking another listener to his story. With his bright eye and skinny hand he must make somebody listen, because what he has to tell is a devastating fear of the utter aloneness of the individual consciousness and he forgets his dread when he has a listener.

Aware of everything only by the treacherous ways of the senses, man has clung to security by fashioning a world of will and reason in which he pursues a common purpose with other men. He and they build a ship and steer it over the sea. They plan a journey, confident that they will find their way home again. Proud of the reason that sets them apart from other creatures, they believe for a brief moment that they are masters of fate and may judge the right and wrong of their conduct. But the ship is enclosed in impenetrable ice and becalmed on a lifeless ocean, and the crew drop down, one by one. If by a chance a mariner returns to his home port, it is not by his own effort but by the will of agencies more powerful than he. At a wedding or in a church he may find a temporary escape from his aloneness, and he has devised sacraments in which he and his goodly fellows appear to be near together. But nothing he can do will ever free him from the constant, unremitting, incalculable portents of the vast sensory world to which he belongs. The will of which he is so proud plays a small part in the train of events that enclose him, and his reason cannot account for even a little of what happens to him. And yet, as he is guided and driven through experiences over which he has no control, he cowers in guilty terror that something he has done may be the cause of his misfortune.

Like that of every living creature, his journey takes place across a world radiant with the light, color, sound and movement in which the senses and the heart take delight. Yet lurking in every flash of light, bright spot of color, seductive motion and angelic sound is a sinister hint of evil. "The bride hath paced into the hall/Red as a rose is she,"—but red, also, are the lips of Life-in-Death, and the footsteps of the bride walking to the altar and the music of the loud bassoon may be unheard in the triumphant whistle of Death's companion. The ice that floats by "green as emerald" is the ice that cracks and growls when it hems the ship in. The luminous mist through which the moonlight peers and the friendly glow of the binnacle-lamp cast a white, ghostly gleam on the face of the steersman. The moon moving softly up the sky has a deceptive loveliness that makes the hot, sultry water of the ocean seem as if covered with the hoar-frost of April. All the way through the tale, there springs on the reader a flash of happy delight in beauty,—the moon in the heavens, the noise "like of a hidden brook/In the leafy month of June," a movement of the body light and effortless as that of a spirit. And then, hard after the shock of the sense of beauty, comes a fear that it is deceitful, for a thick black cloud hangs by the side of the moon, a wicked whisper breaks into prayer, the limbs of the crew are raised like lifeless tools. The strong and pervasive influence on the Mariner of the light, sound and motion that envelop him suspends completely his confidence in reason and will, for, whenever he performs an act as a human being would, it is caught up in a chaos of unwilled movement, and he himself is an alien speck of human purpose tossed meaninglessly about in the roaring wind of fate.

To the Wedding Guests of the world this universe of sensation in which they move is seldom very troublesome and hardly ever suspect. They have been taught to pick and choose and attend to those few of its myriad impressions that are needed for an immediate purpose. On a clear evening they catch sight of the moon, enjoy its light and then turn aside to their task, forgetting that the moon keeps on shining. They hear the skylark sing and

> Sometimes all little birds that are,
> How they seemed to fill the sea and air
> With their sweet jargoning!

—but duty presses on them and they ignore the singing birds. So long as they stay within the narrow confine of conscious thought and purpose, they are able to see and hear only a minute fraction of the impressions continually beating upon them. While their consciousness is busy on its narrow, comfortable routine, their senses store away far more than they know, but even from this tremendous storehouse they may choose only the one or two items they want to remember and, within limits, reject the rest. They hold fast to sanity in the belief that they see what they want to see, move by their own volition and are in command of the direction and purpose of their lives.

The author of "The Ancient Mariner" was far less confident of the power and virtue of the human will and reason. From his child-

hood he was prone to daydreaming, and unbidden fantasies were
more real and vivid than the practical purpose of the day. As he
grew to manhood and found himself oppressed with debt and exam-
inations and the conventional gestures of love-making, he sat down
to brood about fantastic ways of extricating himself instead of taking
the first step to a solution. And the fantasies were always more attractive and vivid than the dull exertion of the will. Into them crept
color and sound and movement that his senses had absorbed from the
world around, and the reveries of daytime and the dreams of sleep
were lit up with the magical brilliance of a sensory world not dimmed
or reduced by the narrow windows of reason. Because he refused to
behave like the common man, looking and then looking away, the
storehouse of his imagination was richly furnished with the light and
sound and motion always pressing in on the mind but often denied
and rejected by a more imperious demand of the will.

A high price is paid, however, for opening the mind freely to
the bright stroke of the sensory world and neglecting the act of
will and reason. Like the Mariner, a man becomes alienated from
the company of other folk and lives alone on an inhuman sea. The
rituals by means of which he tries to forget his isolation,—prayer,
marriage, church-going,—have no longer any but a palliative meaning.
The neighborly acts of pulling at a rope and rowing a boat, in which
the goodly company of human beings engage, appear futile and crazy.
More terrible yet, the brilliance of light and the magic of sound, for
the sake of which the journey from the narrow needs of home is taken,
appear to bear the mark of evil. They lure man to a chaos of sensation
not ruled by the God of the Commandments. In the "green and blue
and white" of the water burn a witch's oils, lovely but sinister, and
all other colors and sounds are alike fascinating and horrible. After
too long a time among these alluring and inhuman sense-impressions,
the soul of man comes back to common living drained of the sap of
humanity, as the Mariner's ship returns to harbor with sere sails and
warped planks.

This is the grim and overpowering conviction with which "The
Ancient Mariner" is saturated and the sad wisdom that the Wedding
Guest awoke to. Henry Nelson Coleridge, having listened to his uncle
talk about the poem, put it quite simply: "the sensitive reader feels
himself insulated, and a sea of wonder and mystery flows round him
as round the spell-stricken ship itself." [4] From this realm of wonder
and mystery the pretty moral lessons that have been read into the
poem are excluded by their very nature, because the realm is one in

[4] *Quarterly Review*, August, 1834.

which act and consequence are unrelated save in mysterious and tragic ways. The doctrines by means of which man tries to persuade himself that the world is subservient to his will and good intentions are rejected one by one,—prayer and sacrifice, kindness and good will, going to a church or to a wedding. To a Sunday School teacher a conclusion of this happy sort may have some value,—"The wisdom gained by the Wedding-Guest is of a positive kind: Love for one's fellow-creatures is a positive blessing and will bring one into closer communion with the God of Nature than any other virtue." [5] In the Mariner's world of accusing eyes, sweating corpses, silent relatives, fiendish looks, it has no place whatsoever. As Coleridge himself said, "In a work of such pure imagination I ought not to have stopped to give reasons for things, or inculcate humanity to beasts," [6] because it is the privilege of the imagination, if it so desires, to lead man away from reason and humanity into an unreasoning and cruel chaos.

On this conviction Coleridge relied constantly, later in his career, for an interpretation of works of imagination that he discussed in his public lectures. In the series of 1818, particularly, the features of the world through which the Mariner moves become those of the imaginative world of the literary artist:

> This is delightfully exemplified in the Arabian Nights' Entertainments. . . . In all these there is the same activity of mind as in dreaming, that is—an exertion of the fancy in the combination and recombination of familiar objects so as to produce novel and wonderful imagery. To this must be added that these tales cause no deep feeling of a moral kind— whether of religion or love; but an impulse of motion is communicated to the mind.[7]

If the reader goes to these tales for familiar pieces of practical and moral instruction, he misses completely the intention of the artist which was not moral or religious at all, but "an impulse of motion," —that quick hurry of the mind from image to image, incident to incident, that occurs when the will and reason relax their control and the direction of the movement is decided by a logic "more subtle, more complex, and dependent on more, and more fugitive causes" than the logic of common sense. Whether any good defense may be made of this activity of the mind is problematical, any more than a reason can be given for the apparently disordered patterns of dream,

---

[5] Elizabeth Nitchie, "The Moral of The Ancient Mariner Reconsidered," *PMLA*, XLVIII (1933), 867–876.

[6] The well-known remark to Mrs. Barbauld in the version of the incident given by H. N. Coleridge in the *Quarterly Review* article above.

[7] *Coleridge's Miscellaneous Criticism*, ed. T. M. Raysor (Cambridge, 1936), p. 193.

but the images seem to justify themselves by their brightness and the swell of emotion on which they move.

In such an activity of the mind he found the cause for the continuing appeal of *Robinson Crusoe*:

> The charm of De Foe's works, especially of Robinson Crusoe, is founded on the same principle. Crusoe himself is merely a representative of humanity in general; neither his intellectual nor his moral qualities set him above the middle degree of mankind; his only prominent characteristic is the spirit of enterprise or wandering, which is, never the less, a very common disposition. You will observe that all that is wonderful in this tale is the result of external circumstances—of things which fortune brings to Crusoe's hand.[8]

The words might have been written about the Mariner or the Wedding Guest, common men both, endowed with a "spirit of enterprise or wandering," prepared to leave the shore of the commonplace for an unknown sea, even if it may be an unknown of terror. To Crusoe as to the Mariner, things happened by chance or fortune, the ordinary rule of cause-and-effect being suspended for the time of the excursion, so that his mind might be laid open to the varied experience of a new world of sense and incident.

On the necessity to lay aside the dominating power of the will, to indulge in a "willing suspension of disbelief for the moment," Coleridge was quite consistent in his theory of literary appreciation. In an earlier lecture of the same series he had talked about *Don Quixote* and the reason for the knight's liking for romances:

> The more remote these romances were from the language of common life, the more akin on that very account were they to the shapeless dreams and strivings of his own mind:—a mind, which possessed not the highest order of genius which lives in an atmosphere of power over mankind, but that minor kind which, in its restlessness, seeks for a vivid representation of its own wishes, and substitutes the movements of that objective puppet for an exercise of actual power in and by itself. The more wild and improbable these romances were, the more were they akin to his will, which had been in the habit of acting as an unlimited monarch over the creations of his fancy.[9]

On the one side, he saw the will as the agent of reason and common sense rigidly controlling the bright patterns of the fancy and subduing them to the common purposes of living. On the other he ranged the might of the imagination to set the fancy free to reflect, in its vivid pictures, the deeper wishes rather than the more immediate

[8] *Ibid.*, p. 194.
[9] *Ibid.*, p. 101.

needs of the heart. Perhaps for the "highest order" of people the ability to impose their will on others and so find happiness was more attractive, but for the common man, the Wedding Guest, restless and unsatisfied in his going to church or to a wedding, an excursion unfettered by will might be an adequate substitute for power.

One hazard of this world of the fancy was that it appeared at times unlimited and without the security of home. This was the burden of the Mariner's woe and of the lesson he taught the Wedding Guest. It was this limitless quality of fancy that Coleridge referred to in his comments on *The Faerie Queene,* and again he brought in the familiar parallel with dream:

> Observe also the exceeding vividness of Spenser's descriptions. They are not, in the true sense of the word, picturesque; but are composed of a wondrous series of images, as in our dreams. . . . You will take especial note of the marvellous independence and true imaginative absence of all particular space or time in the Faery Queene. It is in the domains neither of history or geography; . . . it is truly in the land of Faery, that is, of mental space. The poet has placed you in a dream, a charmed sleep, and you neither wish, nor have the power, to inquire where you are, or how you got there.[10]

Here were included most of the features of this autonomous realm of the fancy on which Coleridge did so much careful brooding,— the vividness of the imagery, the likeness to dream, the suspension of the will and reason, the desire, as he expressed it in a letter, "like the Indian Vishnu, to float about along an infinite ocean cradled in the flower of the Lotus," [11] to be totally and excitingly absorbed in the light, color, and movement of a world removed from the gross and intrusive demand of every day's compulsion.

He recognized, however, that the "phantasmal chaos of association" to which the imagination was indebted for its bright imagery and massive emotion, was not in itself sufficient to create, and over this dilemma he struggled in the *Biographia Literaria.* Daydreaming as a *mere* progression of bright images was not enough for art, as he implied in his condemnation of the novels sent out by the circulating libraries:

> Call it rather a beggarly day-dreaming, during which the mind of the dreamer furnishes for itself nothing but laziness, and a little mawkish sensibility; while the whole *material* and imagery of the dose is supplied *ab extra* by a sort of mental *camera obscura* manufactured at the printing-office, which . . . transmits the moving phantasms of one man's delirium,

[10] *Ibid.,* pp. 35–36.
[11] *Letters,* I, 350.

so as to people the barrenness of a hundred other brains afflicted with the same trance or suspension of all common sense and all definite purpose.[12]

If the needs of the fancy were no more than "a dream world of phantoms and spectres" and a suspension of ordinary will and reason, the cheap novel of the library would be as good as *Don Quixote* or *Robinson Crusoe*. For the ends of common living, the will and reason were in control of the unlicensed crowds of fancy and had to be: "the will, and, with the will, all acts of thought and attention, are . . . distinct powers, the function of which it is to control, determine, and modify the phantasmal chaos of association." [13] Man could not live from day to day in an endless delirium of vivid experience, and "beggarly day-dreaming" was not of itself the source of imaginative power. Yet the point at which the chaos all around and vivid and worthy of the suspension of disbelief, took shape as a work of art was something Coleridge was not able to determine.

He thought he had an answer in the writings of the mystics Jacob Behmen, George Fox, and William Law. Underneath the imagery that filled their writings lay truths of which the images were merely the symbols:

> Need we then be surprised, that, under an excitement at once so strong and so unusual, the man's body should sympathize with the struggles of his mind; or that he should at times be so far deluded, as to mistake the tumultuous sensations of his nerves and the co-existing spectres of his fancy, as parts or symbols of the truths which were opening on him? [14]

The spectres were needed in order to break the mind free from the "lethargy of custom," but the excitement had to arise from deeper sources than a mere holiday of the fancy. Neither was an act of will in itself powerful enough for creation. While it was true that "the will itself by confining and intensifying the attention may arbitrarily give vividness or distinctness to any object whatsoever," [15] this conscious application of the will might also be destructive, limiting and compressing the free play of the fancy. Somewhere, deep within a man, must reside a truth "working unconsciously," one of which he himself might be unaware that in its own hidden way, brought a temporary order into the chaos and, by means of the symbols, made itself apparent. The nearest that Coleridge came to a short statement of

[12] *Biographia Literaria,* ed. Shawcross, I, 34 n.
[13] *Ibid.,* I, 87.
[14] *Ibid.,* I, 97.
[15] *Ibid.,* I, 87.

what he meant was in the remark quoted in Crabb Robinson's *Diary*, that "the imagination under excitement generates and produces a form of its own." It worked in the formless welter of the fancy, using that material because it was brighter and more exciting than the doctrine of the reason, but of these wondrous images it chose only the ones that gave a "vivid representation of its own wishes," a picture of the truth of which it was itself only partly aware.

The simple fact is, of course, that Coleridge, acknowledging wholeheartedly the need for the "spectral" or sensational element in literature, was deadly afraid of its power over him. Whether the sights and sounds with which poetry must be filled came from objects around or from their bright echo in his own mind, he had come to mistrust them and the excitement they kindled. In the Mariner's sea of sensation, his creator, too, felt idle and alone and condemned. During the Alfoxden year, he and Wordsworth kept up an argument on the issue, and neither man could afford to give in. For Wordsworth, who had the power to "confine and intensify" his thinking processes, the world of sense was a blend of Nature and his feelings about it. Out of a "melancholy waste of hopes o'erthrown" he was settling by Dorothy's side into a fruitful period of poetic production, and he struggled with a philosophy to inspire his work. In the quiet of Racedown and Alfoxden, he found in the world of sense and "the common range of visible things" a happiness he had not found in political ideas. From the sights and sounds of Nature he gained a joy and calm secure enough to atone for the desolation of his imprudent years. Knowing what it meant for himself, he came to believe that communion with rivers and mountains was a natural human instinct, and that anyone who bared his heart to Nature was assured of happiness. "Nature," he assured his sister, "never did betray the heart that loved her." Into every piece of verse written when Coleridge and he were neighbors, he poured this consoling theme. Nature was good, and man through his senses could come close to Nature and find, not joy only, but moral guidance.

For a short while he almost made a convert of Coleridge. In one or two poems, "Frost at Midnight," "France: an Ode," "Fears in Solitude," "The Nightingale," Coleridge echoed his friend's philosophy in language not very different from Wordsworth's own. Though he had been "reared in the great city, pent mid cloisters dim" and so had missed the beneficent influence of lakes and mountains and clouds in his childhood, at least his son Hartley would be more blessed and would grow up seeing and hearing "the lovely shapes and sounds intelligible" of the Great Teacher. He agreed with Wordsworth that freedom was not to be found in governments or in political change

but in "earth, sea, and air," when these objects of Nature were regarded with love. He went so far as to find "religious meanings in
the Forms of Nature," and to believe that his heart was softened by
"nature's quietness and solitary musings." In "The Nightingale," a
conversation piece he addressed to William and Dorothy, he was
willing to confess that their lore was also his, and that the voices of
Nature were "always full of love and joyance." It seemed good for the
poet to surrender his spirit "to the influxes/Of shapes and sounds and
shifting elements," [16]—enjoying the moonlight, the song of birds, and
the sight of the evening-star. At the very moment when he described
the wan stars and strange moon presiding over the Mariner's journey
and heard a skylark's song come from the lips of a dead man's spirit,
he was assuring his companion among the combes that these shapes
and sounds were, as Wordsworth wished them to be, the ingredients of
joy.

Yet he was firmly persuaded, as at heart he knew then and was to
declare most firmly later on, that there was no necessary joy for
the heart of man in the world of eye and ear. Wordsworth might
record in the notebook he kept at Alfoxden fragments of verse ex-
tolling the delight of surrendering to the "godlike senses" and laying
"the stirring and inquisitive mind asleep." He could maintain, in a
passage that found its way into *The Excursion,* that

> the man
> Who, in this spirit, communes with the forms
> Of nature, who with understanding heart
> Both knows and loves such objects as excite
> No morbid passions, no disquietude,
> No vengeance, and no hatred—needs must feel
> The joy of that pure principle of love.[17]

He might, more lyrically still, proclaim in "Tintern Abbey" his
love of woods and meadows and mountains and

> of all the mighty world
> Of eye, and ear—both what they half create,
> And what perceive; well pleased to recognize
> In nature and the language of the sense
> The anchor of my purest thoughts, the nurse,
> The guide, the guardian of my heart, and soul
> Of all my moral being.[18]

---

[16] *Poetical Works,* ed. E. H. Coleridge, I, 265–7.

[17] *The Poetical Works of William Wordsworth,* ed. de Selincourt (Oxford, 1940),
IV, 373.

[18] *Ibid.,* II, 262.

Yet the author of "The Ancient Mariner" would never really agree. The objects in the mighty world of the senses were quite prone to excite morbid passions and much disquietude as well as moments of serenity. The eye was not capable, as Wordsworth believed, of speaking "perpetual logic" to the soul because it was innocent of reason and looked on good and evil indifferently. Far from the language of the sense guarding the heart or guiding the moral being, it was packed with images of pain and horror as well as of joy and calm, and it was likely to make evil seductive by the very brilliance of its pictures.

A few years later, the full denial of the doctrine of joy in nature was to come in "Dejection, an Ode":

> I may not hope from outward Forms to win
> The Passion and the Life whose Fountains are within!
> These lifeless Shapes, around, below, above,
> O what can they impart? [19]

But long before, in the world of sense so starkly presented in "The Ancient Mariner," there were few of the blessings that Wordsworth might have found there. From sources too widespread in his reading and experience to be enumerated, Coleridge drew a steady conviction of the peril of relying for happiness on any part of the sensory world. Indiscriminately its objects beat on the windows of the mind. His fancy took them in, treasured them, and built with them the lovely structures of reverie. And, dreaming away the entrusted hours, he felt guilty. By the Clevedon cottage he paid a poet's homage to the white-flowered jasmin and the scents from a nearby bean-field, but Sara's eye reproved him for his indolence. A nightingale heard in the same happy time stirred up a "thousand phantasies," for which he soon began to feel remorseful. In the woods of Alfoxden his friend discovered an arcady safe from the intrusion of human weakness and calamity, but on the same landscape Coleridge noticed a scene of rapine,

> The ivy tod is heavy with snow,
> And the owlet whoops to the wolf below
> That eats the she-wolf's young.

On their walks together, William and Dorothy saw the horned moon, the dim stars and a "great commotion in the air," but theirs was a far happier vision of the scene beneath those bright objects than the lonely plight of the Mariner.

By temperament it was impossible for Coleridge to protect himself

[19] *Letters,* II, 791.

from the shock of the mind's sensibility, as his friend was able to do. He spent days and nights in a constant awareness of "the shifting current in the shoreless chaos of the fancy," with impulses, unsought and unmanageable, breaking in and turning the current this way and that. "Reverie-ish and streamy" by nature, he found his reason impotent to govern the images and feelings that moved ceaselessly across the mirror of his mind. At any moment he was made aware that, a little way beneath the level where will and reason kept a slender grip on practicality, lay a shoreless chaos on which, like the Mariner, he was often adrift. To be abandoned there was madness and ultimate evil:

> During this sleep, or recession of the spirit, the lower, or bestial states of life, rise up into action and prominence. It is an awful thing to be eternally tempted by the perverted senses. The reason may resist—it does resist for a long time; but too often at length, it yields for a moment, and the man is mad for ever! [20]

This he said as an old man in Highgate, but the fear lurking in the words haunted him during most of his adult life.

[20] *Table Talk of Samuel Taylor Coleridge* (London, 1884), May 1, 1830.

PART TWO

View Points

John Livingston Lowes

For the "moral" of the poem, *outside the poem,* will not hold water. It is valid only within that magic circle. The great leap of the voyage from Equator to Equator around the Cape runs true to the chart. But daemons, and spectres, and angels, and *revenants* haunt its course, and the Mariner's voyage, magnificent metamorphosis of fact though it be, can scarcely be regarded as a profitable guide to the fauna of equatorial and arctic seas. The relentless line of cause and consequence runs likewise, unswerving as the voyage, through the poem. But consequence and cause, *in terms of the world of reality,* are ridiculously incommensurable. The shooting of a sea-bird carries in its train the vengeance of an aquatic daemon, acting in conjunction with a spectre-bark; and an impulse of love for other living creatures of the deep summons a troop of angels to navigate an unmanned ship. Moreover, because the Mariner has shot a bird, four times fifty sailors drop down dead, and the slayer himself is doomed to an endless life. The punishment, measured by the standards of a world of balanced penalties, palpably does not fit the crime. But the sphere of balanced penalties is not the given world in which the poem moves. Within *that* world, where birds have tutelary daemons and ships are driven by spectral and angelic powers, consequence and antecedent are in keeping—if for the poet's moment we accept the poet's premises. And the function of the ethical background of "The Ancient Mariner," as Coleridge employs it, is to give the illusion of inevitable sequence to that superb inconsequence. The imaginative use of familiar moral values, like the imaginative use of the familiar outline of a voyage, is leagues away from the promulgation of edifying doctrine through the vehicle of a fairy-tale.

For the very triviality of the act which precipitates its astounding train of consequences is the *sine qua non* of the impression which the poem was intended to convey. The discrepancy is essential to the

From "The Known and Familiar Landscape" by John Livingston Lowes. From The Road to Xanadu (Boston: Houghton Mifflin Co.; London: Constable & Co., Ltd., 1927), pp. 300, 302–3. Copyright © 1927 by John Livingston Lowes. Reprinted by permission of the publishers.

design. And I really know no better short-cut to the comprehension of the poem's unique art than to imagine . . . the substitution of a human being, as the victim, for a bird. A tale the inalienable charm of which (as Coleridge himself perceived) lies in its kinship with the immortal fictions of the *Arabian Nights*, becomes, so motivated, a grotesque and unintelligible caricature of tragedy. Springing from the fall of a feather, it becomes a dome in air, built with music, yet with the shadows of supporting arch and pillar floating midway in the wave. For its world is, in essence, the world of a dream. Its inconsequence is the dream's irrelevance, and by a miracle of art we are possessed, as we read, with that sense of an intimate logic, consecutive and irresistible and more real than reality, which is the dream's supreme illusion. "The events having no necessary consequence do not produce each other," Wordsworth complained in his deplorable strictures on the poem. The events in a dream do not produce each other, but they *seem* to. And that is the sole requirement of the action of the poem.

Frederick A. Pottle

Or, we may say that the poet wins us by imaginative sleight of hand. This appears to be Coleridge's own explanation. Discussing the plans which he and Wordsworth made for the *Lyrical Ballads*, he says that they agreed to attempt two sorts of poems. "In the one, the incidents and agents were to be, in part at least, supernatural; and the excellence aimed at was to consist in the interesting of the affections by the dramatic truth of such emotions, as would naturally accompany such situations, supposing them real. . . . It was agreed, that my endeavours should be directed to persons and characters supernatural, or at least romantic; yet so as to transfer from our inward nature a human interest and a semblance of truth sufficient to procure for these shadows of imagination that willing suspension of disbelief for the moment, which constitutes poetic faith." As the magician, by making us watch his right hand, renders us quite oblivious to what he is doing with his left, so the poet gets us to accept incredible events by keeping our eyes on credible ones. The incredible events are never

From "*Modern Criticism of* The Ancient Mariner" *by Frederick A. Pottle. From Edward J. Gordon and Edward S. Noyes, eds.,* Essays on The Teaching of English (*New York: Appleton-Century-Crofts, 1960*) *pp. 263–64. Copyright © 1960 by The National Council of Teachers of English. Reprinted by permission of The National Council of Teachers of English and the publisher.*

explained or argued about, they just *are*. The concomitants are all of the homely, familiar world. Trivial, sharply realized details, felt instantly to be authentic, pitch us directly into incredible ones [ll. 203–211]. No ordinary Gothic would have found a place for the blanched face of the steersman or the dew dripping from the sails; but nothing could more effectively sap our defenses against the horror of that moon with its impossible star. The causal relation of events is accepted as adequate because the Mariner accepts it as adequate. The morality does not shock us, because, though Coleridge has given it an avowedly Christian basis, he has presented the story dramatically through the lips of a medieval, superstitious, and possibly deranged old man. It is, after all, not unlike a story from the Old Testament recording the exceeding fierce wrath of the Lord; for example, how he smote the men of Bethshemesh because, through no malice at all, they had looked into the ark; "even he smote of the people fifty thousand and threescore and ten men: and the people lamented." The poem runs the gamut of genuine guilt and remorse, suffering and consolation, hate and forgiveness, grief and joy. Since the emotions are so true to universal human experience, we accept the events that are advanced as their cause.

Maud Bodkin

I will now attempt, focusing upon that "great stanza" with its contrast of white moonlight and red shadow, to give something of what I find to be the experience communicated.

In following the description of the Mariner's vigil upon the stagnant sea, it is not till I come to this stanza that I recognize an image detaching itself spontaneously and strongly from the synthetic grasp of the poem's meaning. I live in the Mariner's anguish of repulsion— from the rotting deck where lay the dead, and rotting sea and slimy creatures—with no discernible image at all, other than the voice speaking with inflexions of despair, and the faint organic changes that go with such inflexions—unless, of course, I demand an image. When I did that on one occasion, there appeared an image of a crowd of people struggling for a bus at a particular London street corner. For

From "*A Study of 'The Ancient Mariner' and of the Rebirth Archetype*" by *Maud Bodkin.* From Archetypal Patterns in Poetry: Psychological Studies of Imagination (*London: Oxford University Press, 1934*), *pp. 43–45, 46–48, 81.* Copyright © *1934* by *Oxford University Press. Reprinted by permission of the publisher.*

a moment I thought the numerical suggestion in the "thousand thousand slimy things" had broken right away from its context; but then, catching the atmosphere of my street-corner image, I recognized the mood of shrinking disgust that had operated in calling up the picture.

With the transition from the Mariner's utter despair to his yearning vision of the moon in its soft journeying through the sky, there comes a stirring of images which, however, do not emerge spontaneously from out the magic of the charged verse; but when I come to the lines that lead from the white-moonlight to the "huge shadow" of the ship where the water burns red, the emotional stress upon that colour-word has become so intense that an image breaks out from it of a red that burns downward through shadow, as into an abyss. . . . The word "red" has a soul of terror that has come to it through the history of the race. . . . It is—for me, at least—the same soul that is evoked from the word "red" in Coleridge's stanza and in Dante's lines; and thus— to my feeling—it is as though the Mariner, his deliverance just begun through the power of the moon's beauty, for the moment falls again to Hell in the red shadow of the ship.

Let us pass now to the storm—the roaring wind and streaming rain and lightning, by which the stagnant calm and drought is broken, when the Mariner's impulse of love has undone the curse that held both him and Nature transfixed. [ll. 313–326]

Lowes has traced passages in the Voyages known to have been studied by Coleridge, which describe tropical or subtropical storms —for instance, a description from Bartram, of torrential rain that obscured every object, "excepting the continuous streams or rivers of lightning pouring from the clouds." Such lightning, he remarks, Coleridge has pretty certainly never seen in Devon or Somerset, but he had seen it "in those ocular spectra of his which kept pace with his reading."

Lowes traces to passages read by Coleridge not only the lightning, but the more obscure references to "fire flags" and the "wan stars" seen through the auroral lights; and we may gratefully acknowledge the interest of the glimpses his researches give of the transmutation into poetry of scattered fragments of travellers' tales. Yet here again, it seems to me we must add to what he tells us insight from our own experience into the emotional forces that are the agents of the transmutation. I would ask the reader who has dwelt upon these storm stanzas of Coleridge, and felt that in his mind they take, as it were, a place shaped and prepared for them, how would he account for such sense of familiarity. In my own mind the streaming rain and lightning of the poem is interrelated with storms felt and seen in dreams. Fading impressions of such rain and lightning recalled on waking have clothed themselves in the flowing words of the poem and become fused with these.

Is it again the racial mind or inheritance, active within the individual sensibility, whether of Coleridge or of his reader, that both assimilates the descriptions of tropical storms, and sees in a heightened pattern those storms of our own country that "startle" and overpower, and "send the soul abroad"? It was, I think, of a Sussex storm, "marching in a dark breastplate and in the skirts of rain, with thunders about it," that Belloc wrote. . . .

The thought of the storm image, and the place it has held in the mind, not of Europe only but of a wider, older culture, takes us back to that order of conception, illustrated already in reference to wind and spirit, wherein the two aspects we now distinguish, of outer sense impression and inly felt process, appear undifferentiated. Dr. Jung cites from the Vedic Hymns lines where prayers, or ritual fire-boring, are said to lead forth, or release, the flowing streams of Rita; and shows that the ancient idea of Rita represented, in undifferentiated fashion, at once the cycle of nature of which rain and fire are offspring, and also the ritually ordered processes of the inner life, in which pent-up energy can be discharged by fitting ceremonial.

The storm which for the experiencing mind appears not as differentiated physical object but as a phase of its own life, is naturally thought of as let loose by prayer, when prayer transforms the whole current and atmosphere of the inner life. In Coleridge's poem the relief of rain follows the relaxing of the inner tension by the act of love and prayer, as naturally and inevitably as deep sleep and healing dreams. [ll. 297–304]

We accept the sequence with such feeling as that with which we accept the narration in terms of recognized metaphor, of a psychical sequence of emotional energy-tension and release—as when, for example, we are told by St. Augustine in his *Confessions* of the long anxiety and suspense that preceded his conversion, and how, when reflection had "gathered up and heaped together all my misery in the sight of my heart, a mighty storm arose, bringing a mighty shower of tears."

In the present essay I have examined the experience communicated by *The Ancient Mariner*, seeking to maintain such a standard of sincerity of response, and availing myself of a method suggested partly by that of medical analysts, inspired also by a positive ideal of sincerity in seeking to overcome obstacles to self-knowledge.

I have presented tentatively, to the judgement of others who care to examine and compare their own experience of the poem, a conclusion concerning the psychological or spiritual relations it communicates—relations not easily detached for separate consideration from the total experience of the poem, but which we may recall in some such form as this: that the beauty of life is revealed amid the slime, that the glory of life is renewed after stagnation, that through the power of speech the values achieved by life are made immortal.

Samuel Taylor Coleridge

Mrs. Barbauld once told me that she admired the Ancient Mariner very much, but that there were two faults in it,—it was improbable, and had no moral. As for the probability, I owned that that might admit some question; but as to the want of a moral, I told her that in my own judgment the poem had too much; and that the only or chief fault, if I might say so, was the obtrusion of the moral sentiment so openly on the reader as a principle or cause of action in a work of such pure imagination. It ought to have had no more moral than the Arabian Nights' tale of the merchant's sitting down to eat dates by the side of a well, and throwing the shells aside, and lo! a geni starts up, and says he *must* kill the aforesaid merchant, *because* one of the date-shells had, it seems, put out the eye of the geni's son.

From Table Talk of Samuel Taylor Coleridge *in* Complete Works of Samuel Taylor Coleridge (*New York: Harper & Bros., 1856*) , *VI, 324.*

Chronology of Important Dates

	Coleridge	Historical and Cultural Activities
1772	Coleridge born.	
1775-89		American War of Independence.
1789		Fall of the Bastille.
1791-94	Coleridge sizar and scholar, Jesus College, Cambridge.	French Revolution. Reign of Terror. Anti-Jacobin trials of Liberals in England.
1798	"The Rime of the Ancient Mariner" published in *Lyrical Ballads.*	Rise of Napoleon. Beginning of Napoleonic Wars (1798–1815).
1802	"Dejection: An Ode" published in *Morning Post.*	
1805		Nelson's victory at Trafalgar.
1810-12	Break with Wordsworth. Lectures on Shakespeare.	American War of 1812. Napoleon's Russian campaign.
1815		Battle of Waterloo.
1816	"Christabel" published. Move to Highgate.	Reaction and Tory control in England until 1830.
1817	*Biographia Literaria* and *Sibylline Leaves* published.	Widespread depression, social disorder, and repression in England to 1828.
1825	*Aids to Reflection* published.	

1829	*On the Constitution of the Church and State* published.	Catholic Emancipation Act passed.
1832		First Reform Bill passed. Sir Walter Scott dies.
1834	Coleridge dies at Highgate, July 25.	

Notes on the Editor and Contributors

JAMES D. BOULGER is Associate Professor of English at Brown University. He has published *Coleridge as Religious Thinker* (1961) and articles on the Romantic Poets.

MAUD BODKIN, in addition to *Archetypal Patterns in Poetry* (1934), has published *Studies of Type Images on Poetry, Religion, and Philosophy* (1951) and articles in British journals of psychology and literature.

A. M. BUCHAN is Professor Emeritus of English, Washington University, St. Louis, Mo.

HUMPHRY HOUSE (d. 1955) was Senior Lecturer in English at Wadham College, Oxford. In addition to *Coleridge: The Clark Lectures* (1953), he edited *The Notebooks and Papers of Gerard Manley Hopkins* (1937).

JOHN LIVINGSTON LOWES (1867–1945) was Professor of English at Harvard University. In addition to *The Road to Xanadu* (1927), he wrote *The Art of Geoffrey Chaucer* (1931) and numerous articles on the Medieval period.

FREDERICK A. POTTLE is Professor Emeritus of English at Yale University, and the general editor of the Yale editions of the private papers of James Boswell.

ROBERT PENN WARREN, noted poet, novelist, and critic, is Professor of writing and drama at Yale University.

GEORGE WHALLEY is Professor of English at Queens University, Kingston, Ontario. He has written *Coleridge, Sara Hutchinson, and the Asra Poems* (1955), and is editing the *Marginalia* and *Poems* in the forthcoming *Collected Coleridge* (general editor, Kathleen Coburn).

Selected Bibliography

Bald, R. C., "Coleridge and *The Ancient Mariner*: Addenda to *The Road to Xanadu*," *Nineteenth Century Studies.* Cornell, 1940. Pp. 1–45.

Beer, J. B., *Coleridge the Visionary.* London, Chatto & Windus, 1959. Chapter V, "The Glorious Sun," pp. 133–74 on "The Ancient Mariner." Entire book recommended.

Bodkin, Maud, *Archetypal Patterns in Poetry: Psychological Studies of Imagination.* London: Oxford University Press, 1934. Chapter II recommended: "A Study of 'The Ancient Mariner' and of the Rebirth Archetype," pp. 26–89.

Bostetter, Edward, "The Nightmare World of *The Ancient Mariner*," *Studies in Romanticism*, I (Summer, 1962), pp. 241–54.

Brett, R. L., "Coleridge's 'The Rime of The Ancient Mariner,' " Chapter Four in *Reason and Imagination: A Study of Form and Meaning in Four Poems.* London: Oxford University Press, 1960. Pp. 78–107.

Gose, Elliott B., "Coleridge and the Luminous Gloom," *PMLA*, LXXV (June, 1960), 238–44.

Harding, D. W., "The Theme of 'The Ancient Mariner,' " *Scrutiny*, IX (March, 1941), 334–42. Reprinted in *Experience into Words.* London: Chatto & Windus, Ltd., 1963.

Lowes, J. L., *The Road to Xanadu.* Boston: Houghton Mifflin Co., 1927. Entire book recommended.

Schulz, Max F., *The Poetic Voices of Coleridge.* Detroit: Wayne State University Press, 1963. Chap. IV, "The Ventriloquism Voice," pp. 51–71.

TWENTIETH CENTURY
INTERPRETATIONS

MAYNARD MACK, *Series Editor*
YALE UNIVERSITY

NOW AVAILABLE
Collections of Critical Essays
ON